THE MAKING OF
LICENCE TO KILL

THE MAKING OF
LICENCE TO KILL

SALLY HIBBIN

HAMLYN

Published in 1989
by The Hamlyn Publishing Group Limited
a division of The Octopus Publishing Group,
Michelin House, 81 Fulham Road, London SW3 6RB

ISBN 0 600 56352 9

Printed in Great Britain

Photographic acknowledgments
All photographs © 1988, 1989 Danjaq S.A. and United Artists
Company.
All rights reserved.
Designed by Ran Barnes

Also available from Hamlyn

THE NEW OFFICIAL JAMES BOND 007 MOVIE BOOK

The revised edition of the best-selling official story of 27 years
of James Bond 007 films produced by Eon Productions. Includes the
latest James Bond 007 blockbuster, *Licence to Kill*, revised section
on *The Living Daylights* and a complete, comprehensive credits
listing for all James Bond 007 movies
UK Price £6.95   Softback   ISBN 0 600 56352 9

THE OFFICAL JAMES BOND 007 MOVIE POSTER BOOK

Reissued with a pull-out giant-size movie poster of the latest 007
film, *Licence to Kill*, this is the ultimate souvenir for all Bond
fans, featuring full-page colour poster artworks of all the Eon
Productions 007 films, from *Dr No* to *The Living Daylights*.
48 pages. 20 colour artworks.
UK Price £5.95   Softback   ISBN 0 600 55315 9

CONTENTS

FOREWORD

'I know its a cliché,' said Barbara Broccoli, one day in Mexicali, 'but the Bond films are like a family.' And, with many of the same team involved in each new Bond film, working and living together for at least six months every two years, it is certainly true. I was privileged, for a few weeks during the shooting of *Licence to Kill*, to be taken in as part of the family and given access to the cast and crew of the film.

This would not have been possible without the co-operation of the crew, many of whom deeply distrust members of the press and have all been 'burnt' on previous occasions. I am grateful to them for, nevertheless,

including me as part of the crew, talking to me and giving me the information and anecdotes necessary for writing this book.

I would also like to thank Jerry Juroe and Saul Cooper for their help and patience, strained at times, with my many requests; to unit photographers Keith Hamshere and George Whitear who introduced me to their respective units and looked after me until I found my feet; and to Amanda Schofield at Eon's London offices.

The atmosphere on the Bond films is very relaxed and I thoroughly enjoyed researching this book. I hope you get as much from reading it.

INTRODUCTION

For nearly three decades, James Bond has been delighting audiences with his stylish adventures, going from film to film, never failing to entertain old fans or win new ones. *Licence to Kill* is the 16th Bond film in the ever-popular series and at the head of the team sits Albert R. 'Cubby' Broccoli.

He has been a producer of the films since the very beginning, at first in partnership with Harry Saltzman, then on his own, and more recently with Michael G. Wilson. From the early days of *Dr No*, through four actors playing the central role and several different directors, 'Cubby' has remained the guiding light of the 007 films.

To what does 'Cubby' attribute the phenomenal worldwide success of the series? 'We have a good subject: James Bond, 007. That's the real secret. Whether Roger or Sean or Timothy or somebody else plays Bond, the symbol is there. And people react to that. The audience figures are very high on 007. We've always had our competitors so we try to bring something new to the screen each time.'

The formula – combining action, glamour, technology and humour – certainly works, for, over the years, a staggering 1.75 billion have paid for cinema admissions to see the 15 Bond films. And with chart-topping TV showings and video sales, it is estimated that over half the world's population has seen a Bond film at one time or another.

'It's a challenge we've been facing for some 27 years,' 'Cubby' continued. 'I guess our success is through luck primarily because we haven't any great intuition and aren't particularly clever,' he added modestly. 'It's difficult and gets more so each time. Things change, we have to feel our way through what the public expects intuitively because it is the public we want to please. It's when the picture hits the screen and the public react favourably that we get our pay off.'

'Cubby' has always been commit-

Above: *'Cubby' Broccoli opens the shooting by slating the first take of the film. The clapperboard has the original title,* Licence Revoked *(with the American spelling) on it. The title was changed – to* Licence to Kill *– when it was feared that too many people would question the meaning of 'revoked'.*

Below: *Timothy Dalton, in his second film of the series, strikes the classic James Bond pose.*

ted to making Bonds family entertainment, using all the elements that audiences have come to know and look for in each successive Bond film: the erotic, glowing main titles; the spectacular ski, boat or car chases; the beautiful underwater sequences; the pacy soundtracks; the up-to-the-minute title song rendered by a popular artist; the fantastic sets; the endless seductions of glamorous women and, of course, the distinctive Bond humour.

But with Timothy Dalton in the lead, the films have changed to suit a more thoughtful audience. 'Over the years, we have been really careful to make films that the audience – the families – would appreciate. Now we would like to react in a slightly more realistic way. We still won't show, however, nudity in deference to that family audience. The kids are way ahead of us – they know more about what's going on than we do. So in this film we might be a little bit bolder, catering a little bit more for an adult audience than we have done previously.'

It is difficult to imagine how 'Cubby' maintains his enthusiasm for 007 after so many years. But he soon dispels any idea that he has become tired with it all. 'I feel I have an obligation to the people who

Right: *John Glen (seated on the left) with the camera crew.*

have made a success of James Bond – people whom I've worked with over the years and who enjoy working for us. I enjoy working with them because they're a good group of people and we've made it together.

'My commitment to Bond does deprive me of the opportunity of doing other films. Obviously at times I have regretted being tied down to making just Bonds, nevertheless I keep on doing it. I have many dreams and many ideas but I also have a feeling of responsibility to all the people who are waiting for each new one to come out. And they are still flocking to see the films, so we carry on making them.'

As time has gone by, so the costs of film production have risen dramatically and 'Cubby' is keenly aware of the need for the Bond films to be competitively priced if they are to survive. 'The first Bond film was budgeted at $1 million. Today that does not even pay the print costs, everything has gone so sky high.'

This time, rising costs led to a move away from England and Pinewood Studios, 'our home away from home,' according to 'Cubby'. But he is philosophical about the change. 'My father used to say to me, "He

who looks for a new rather than an old way, knows what he's leaving but he does not know what he's going to find," and that's what happens with us. We left England to find a cheaper way of making our films and we found a lot of problems in Mexico. So making a film today is not easy.'

Once the script and budget are agreed, 'Cubby' fulfils his responsibility to the investors to bring the picture in as close to the projected cost as possible. His role in the making of the Bond films is, however, far more than a technical one. There is a tremendous loyalty between 'Cubby' and his crew that

leads to an unusually relaxed and family atmosphere on the set.

' 'Cubby' has always encouraged that feeling,' commented Michael G. Wilson, his co-producer. 'It's his style. In a business where there is not much of that attitude around, it seems to be appreciated by the crew.'

'Cubby' is equally aware of this. 'We've got a good crew. I am the old father figure to them and they may feel a little more secure if I'm there. They know they can get the job done without interference.'

The special, close, family feel of the Bond set is accentuated by the fact that many of 'Cubby's' own family work on the films. 'I am proud of my family: my daughters, my stepson. They're not being paid a phenomenal amount of money and they are doing a better job than I expected.'

Remarkably, this family feeling is welcomed by newcomers to the films, not resented. New Bond girl, Talisa Soto, was very impressed with the warmth of the family feeling around her, comparing it to 'old Hollywood'. 'It makes you feel special,' she said.

Carey Lowell, James Bond's new leading lady, added her comment, 'Everyone's done it together so long, they're really accepting of newcomers. 'Cubby's' family is James Bond.'

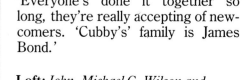

Left: *John, Michael G. Wilson and 'Cubby' Broccoli on location.*
Right: *The teaser poster for the film.*

CREATING THE NEW BOND

The exciting climactic chase of Licence to Kill *is pure Bond adventure with giant trucks performing a variety of tricks including this hair-raising 'wheelie' in which a truck bucks on its back wheels like a horse.*

CHANGING THE IMAGE

Over the years, the Bond films have created a certain tradition, a way of telling a stylish adventure story with particular well-known and well-loved elements. Each film takes a different approach, but many of the aspects remain essentially the same – and that is half the fun for the audience, waiting to see how once again, Bond foils the enemy and comes out on top. Everyone knows that a Bond film will contain exotic locales, beautiful women and spectacular stunts. These are the standard components. What is new is the way these threads are spun together to create an exciting and pacy thriller.

Richard Maibaum has been involved with the Bond films since *Dr No*. He has scripted, often in association with others, twelve of them and collaborated on the writing of *Licence to Kill* with Michael G. Wilson. He has a very clear understanding of the aim of a Bond story. 'In the past our films were not real. We were not trying to portray reality in any sense of the word. We were a fantasy and we were never worried about that. It just depended on how we involved people in that fantasy –what the world was in which they found themselves.

'I'm very proud of being a long-runner on the Bonds. I think we brought something new to films and started a trend. It was a new way of telling a story. Now they all copy James Bond but give it a different wrinkle. And we did it without resorting to cheap displays of nudity and without being vulgar. Our technique is to skirt between fantasy and reality so that you get the best of all possible worlds. It's not so serious and logical as other films, it even comes close to the illogical which makes it surprising. 'Cubby' used to say, "amaze me". I have tried to do that – I haven't always succeeded. But at its best, it produces an effect the audience has not experienced before. It becomes a fable – yet it remains lifelike. That is the real trick.'

The scriptwriters have now run out of Fleming novels, not that these have recently been considered as anything more than starting points for successive films. They have used the titles and some of the incidents but little else. 'You have to think what has not been done, what kind of characters we could have. We don't want to repeat anything except what the audience wants.'

Michael G. Wilson, who co-wrote and produced *Licence to Kill*, agreed with Richard. 'There is a problem of not changing too much. Bond has a certain formula, a style, and you don't want to disappoint the audience and their expectations. On the other hand you can't be too predictable or it would be disastrous.'

'We find a character,' Richard explained, 'and start asking questions. One thing leads to another and eventually, after a great deal of talking and arguing, a story emerges.' *Licence to Kill* started with two 1960-published short stories of Fleming's entitled *The Hildebrand Rarity* and *For Your Eyes Only* published as part of the *Octopussy* collection. Krest was one of the characters, a real villain who winds up dead with a fish in his mouth. 'We liked the character and created a story around him,' Richard said.

At this stage, Michael and Richard discuss the general idea with 'Cubby' Broccoli. If he likes the concept then the other central member of the Bond team, director John Glen, joins in. Richard and Michael present their proposals and everyone kicks them about. They travel around looking for ideas, talk about a few different treatments, start spinning yarns and finally come up with one that they all like. This time around, they began by thinking about exotic, unfamiliar locations in China and travelled out there during November and December 1987. Eventually, they decided to look in a different direction.

Robert Davi plays Franz Sanchez, the most modern of the Bond villains. He is a Latin American drug lord with a chillingly menacing plan for expanding his empire.

'We could not come up with a China story that was right for us,' explained Michael. 'It turned out to be too expensive and we were left high and dry,' Richard added. John Glen put it differently. 'We thought China would be a novel place to shoot. But then *The Last Emperor* (1988) came out and took the edge off the idea. It turned out to be a very expensive country and the distances were vast. There were wonderful locations but so widely spread out. People were very helpful and kind and perhaps we will go back there some day.'

By January, they were searching the Caribbean, looking for suitable islands. They finally decided on Key West, Florida – it was not as expensive as most Caribbean locations, yet it is exotic with the right atmosphere for a smuggling story.

The fact that suggestions made by all sorts of people associated with the film are considered and often incorporated, demonstrates the family feeling of the Bond films. This is particularly true of the stunts. 'You start with a situation and figure out what would be exciting,' said Michael G. Wilson. The opening sequence of *Licence to Kill*, for instance, was the result of much discussion, back and forth between 'Cubby', John and the writers. On the other hand, the climactic truck sequence was an idea that John Glen had been thinking over for a number of years.

No one on the Bond crew ever says, 'This is impossible'; they just work out how to do it. And, as often as not, the stunts do not depend upon optical effects created and produced in the laboratory. 'We are more creative about our stunts,' explained John. 'We find a means of doing them for real without it being dangerous.' It is in many ways a simple style without the modern high-tech wizardry so common today, and that is part of the charm of the films

When the discussions are over, it is once again up to the writers to pull it all together. 'When all is said and done,' Richard Maibaum concluded, 'when all the suggestions are in, the writer's got to put the damn thing down.

Michael G. Wilson and Richard Maibaum were working on *Licence to Kill* when Richard had to withdraw from the film when the Writers' Guild of America went on strike. Richard was upset about not being able to continue with the series he was so close to. 'It was torture for me to sit through 22 weeks wondering what's going on. I've done 23 films for 'Cubby' and had split loyalties but I had to follow my Guild. And, in the end, the writers made the point that they are a force to be reckoned with.'

Timothy Dalton and Michael G. Wilson discuss a plot point between takes. They are sitting on the balcony of the Hemingway House in Key West, where the crucial confrontation between Bond and M takes place in the film.

PROFILE

Name: Timothy Dalton

Alias: James Bond (007)
Job description: secret agent with a licence to kill.
Bond history: *The Living Daylights, Licence to Kill*

Although Timothy Dalton was born in Colwyn Bay, North Wales, he is of English parentage. He began his training at the National Youth Theatre following it up with attendance at RADA. It was essentially a classical training and, like many an aspiring actor, he gained a wide range of experience in the theatre, his first love, both in repertory and on the London stage, tackling everything from Shakespeare to Shaffer. He is proud of his stage work, which he has always continued despite a thriving film career, and wants to do more.

Most recently, he won critical acclaim when he co-starred with Vanessa Redgrave in *A Touch of the Poet*, a Eugene O'Neill play which he was responsible for bringing to London's West End for the first time. 'It is a major play by one of the 20th century's greatest playwrights, and we've put it right back on the theatrical map,' he told me. 'I was very proud of it. We've been asked to take it to Broadway.'

His dark, sleek, almost smouldering looks, led to a film career, mainly as a romantic figure in historical fiction. He played the young King of France in *The Lion in Winter* (1968) alongside Peter O'Toole and Katharine Hepburn, tackled Rochester in the television series *Jane Eyre*, was Heathcliff in *Wuthering Heights* (1970) and Darnley in *Mary, Queen of Scots* (1971). More recently, he starred in *Agatha* (1978), *Flash Gordon* (1980) and *The Doctor and the Devils* (1985).

When asked to take on the role of James Bond, he grasped the opportunity, wishing to play the famous secret agent in the way Fleming intended. 'He obviously did something right. They were great best-sellers and still are. I was astonished to discover just how good a read they are even today. He created the character of James Bond and he did it right.'

In between *The Living Daylights* and *Licence to Kill*, he starred with Anthony

Edwards (from the highly successful hit *Top Gun* and the recent *Mr North* (1989)) in a two-hander, *Hawks* (1988). Many of the Bond crew worked on that film with Timothy and it was clearly a project they all enjoyed. 'It is about a couple of ordinary guys who are in remission from cancer. The subject of the film is how they tackle life with courage and humour in the face of an uncertain future and the human values which they learn from their shared experience.'

So how does Timothy, who is always in demand, decide which projects to take on? 'I look for value. But it is a very relative term. There is a tremendous amount of variety in what you're asked to do. Bond is a valuable film because it brings a great deal of pleasure and excitement and entertainment on a fantsay level. There are other projects which bring other values in different ways. If it's good work and I think I can bring something to it, then I would seriously consider doing it.'

AFTER *MOONRAKER*

Moonraker took the Bond series into outer space with space age jokes and space battles. It was the height of the tongue-in-cheek Roger Moore period of the series and the film did very well at the box office. It was also the most expensive Bond to date. When John Glen took over the direction with the next film, *For Your Eyes Only*, a deliberate change of style took place. 'We had gone as far as we could into space,' John explained. 'We needed a change of some sort, back to the grass roots of Bond. We wanted to make the new film more of a thriller than a romp, without losing sight of what made Bond famous – its humour.'

'With *Moonraker*,' Richard said, 'we went too far in the outlandish. The audience did not believe any more and Roger spoofed too much.' When Timothy Dalton was brought in as the new Bond, the films were free to consolidate the change of direction. 'When I was asked about doing Bond,' Timothy recalled,

'there was a clear directive from Mr Broccoli that he wanted the films to try and recapture something of the spirit of the early ones – *From Russia With Love, Goldfinger*. Those were the films that I'd liked the best and which I thought came nearest to recapturing the spirit of the Fleming books. They are all escapist fantasies but like any good fantasy, you've got to become involved in them to enjoy them, to suspend your disbelief and believe, and within that framework both the books and the early films were believable. That's why I said I'd like to do them – because that framework was there for me to operate in. How they will develop, only time will tell.'

'I personally didn't feel it was enough to go back to the original formula,' John added, 'but I wanted to take it a stage further and with Timothy we have an actor who can do it. *Licence to Kill* is written for Timothy – the first film written for him as *The Living Daylights* was only

adapted for him. This means we can have far more action, because Timothy does it so well.'

'We could not do the same stories with Timothy as with Roger,' Michael continued. 'We have to adapt. With Timothy we are closer to the Fleming style. Timothy wants to create a character that's much more human, more realistic. The films then play a bit tougher. Roger played a sophisticated, tongue-in-cheek style. I hope Timothy is the next generation. First time out people are curious, second time they have to come back, deliberately.'

Richard, too, liked the new emphasis. 'I'm very pleased to see the move towards more gritty reality. If the actor does not believe what's happening, the audience will not believe it either and Timothy certainly has the ability to take the audience with him.'

In his own domain, Sanchez' power is absolute – even over his woman, Lupe (played by Taliso Soto). He will not tolerate her looking at any other man, especially one who is in his pay.

PROFILE

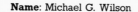

Name: Michael G. Wilson

Bond history: *The Spy Who Loved Me* (assistant to the producer), *Moonraker* (executive producer), *For Your Eyes Only* (executive producer, scriptwriter), *Octopussy* (executive producer, scriptwriter), *A View to a Kill* (producer, scriptwriter), *The Living Daylights* (producer, scriptwriter), *Licence to Kill* (producer, scriptwriter).

Michael G. Wilson has two roles with the Bond movies these days. He co-writes the scripts and he co-produces the film itself. He is, as such, one of the most central figures in the creation of each new Bond film.

But Michael, despite being 'Cubby' Broccoli's stepson did not begin life in the film industry. He graduated from college as an electrical engineer and then moved into law, specializing in international taxation. He joined Eon Productions on the legal side in 1972, earning the credit of the assistant to the producer on *The Spy Who Loved Me* and rising to executive producer on *Moonraker*. It was no surprise to those who knew him when this multi-talented man began to be intimately involved in the writing of the films as well.

He was instrumental in the change of direction introduced with *For Your Eyes Only* and has had a major part in writing the film scripts since. He may joke that once filming starts, all he does is 'stand around' but he is with the film every minute of the day, constantly solving problems or making final, crucial adjustments to the script.

He is also an accomplished stills photographer with a unique collection of rare photographs which he lends to museums around the world. The collection, one of the world's largest, has its own curator.

LICENCE TO KILL

John Glen and his assistant director, Miguel Gil, rehearse a scene in the casino with Timothy Dalton.

As John Glen pointed out, *Licence to Kill* is tailored to Timothy Dalton. 'We know our man and his capabilities and we can utilize his unique style of acting. He has an edge, a hardness, but at the same time he can develop relationships.'

The story they developed was one straight out of the news headlines: a hard-hitting adventure inspired by the arrest of a Bolivian drug dealer who was brought to the States for trial. 'This Bond is probably a much tougher Bond than we've ever done in the series,' commented John. 'There's more bloodshed but at the same time the story gives Bond a very strong motivation to avenge the maiming of Felix Leiter, his life-long friend. Because of this and the fact that he's up against such an evil opponent, he has the opportunity to be very hard. He's driven on by the desire to avenge his friend and becomes a man on the run. The light relief is provided by Q who has by far the biggest part he's ever had and he's risen to it admirably.'

During the filming there was much speculation about what certificate *Licence to Kill* would receive. An 18 certificate in England would be a first. Is there a danger of moving away from the traditional audience? 'Censorship is a moving target,' Michael explained. 'Attitudes vary from time to time in different countries, so you make the best film you can and deal with the censors later.'

Losing his 'licence to kill' gives Bond a rare opportunity to break out of his traditional role. Released from the harness of the secret service, he is free to feel emotion, anger, revenge. In acting terms, it is possibly the most challenging part that has yet been written for Bond and Timothy Dalton is easily equal to it.

Timothy, who has read all the Fleming novels and seen all the Bond films, is very clear about the kind of person that 007 really is. 'The interesting thing about the Bond of the Fleming books, which I think Sean Connery got hold of extraordinarily well in spirit, is that he is in a way a writer's paradox. Fleming could write about a man who was ruthless and hard, a thorough professional, absolutely capable of carrying out his assignment but at the same time he could, through his writing, give this complex char-

acter an awareness, sensibility, cynicism and what he referred to as "accidie", this distaste with the nastiness of his job.

'The real everyday world of spies, of killing people, of treachery is nasty. Fleming didn't really like it and I think he made Bond not really like it either. It is surprising the number of books in which Bond is totally unenthusiastic about the world in which he lives. But then Fleming gives him a very clear-cut enemy, evil in a mythical sense, and that immediately takes Bond out of whatever mood he's in and makes him a force fighting for good. It is a worldwide, obvious sense of evil. It's fascinating to see Bond being afraid, like any normal person would be: to see him being brutal where necessary and it's also good to see his sensitivity challenged. It makes him human. You can't relate to a

superhero, to a superman, but you can identify with a real man who in times of crisis draws forth some extraordinary quality from within himself and triumphs but only after a struggle. Real courage is knowing what faces you and knowing how to face it.'

Timothy is understandably reluctant to compare the actors who have played James Bond over the years. 'The movies seem to me to have followed, in a broad sense, two different styles. The first Bonds were adventure thrillers, the later ones were technological extravaganzas with a light comedic style. They were a completely different approach so the tasks that faced Sean Connery and Roger Moore were completely different.'

Richard Maibaum, however, saw the continuity in the character as well as the changes. 'I have always tried to see James Bond as personally charming, witty and understanding. He is brutal when necessary but

Above: *Q (Desmond Llewelyn) is, more than ever, involved in the action – and the lighter side of* Licence to Kill. *He is seen here as Bond's chauffeur in Isthmus City.*

Left: *The tanker chase is one of the highlights of the film. The tankers are used by Sanchez to transport his drugs, using a new technique which mixes cocaine and gasoline. The two substances are later separated out in his laboratory. The tanker sequence is not only exciting it also exactly captures the mood of the new gritty Bond.*

gentle when he wants to be. Connery gave an ingrained Scottish irony to the part – what I refer to as pulling down the balloon. You get a fantastic piece of action followed by a wisecrack which acts as a sort of safety valve. Humour is a wonderful common denominator. And, in this film, we take more advantage than formerly of Desmond Llewelyn's wonderful deadpan delivery.'

THE DIRECTION

From script to screen, the film is in the hands of director John Glen. He places his emphasis on the visual aspects of Bond, an exciting, pacy, stimulating style that never stands still but continually changes and challenges. 'The action content of the films,' he contended, 'which we have never lost sight of, is international. It transcends language barriers because it is so visual.'

John gets involved very early on, at outline stage of the film, particularly developing the action scenes. 'I like to exploit every possibility within the parameters of the idea. We never like to copy or repeat, and always make the action original each time. For instance, if we have a car chase, it has to be done differently from how it is seen everyday on television.' He is also very aware of the comic possibilities of the action, recognizing that much of the humour occurs in those sequences.

He is the kind of director who knows how to make the money go where he wants it. 'You have to put weight on certain areas of the film and spend the money on those shots. In other words, you spend money on what makes Bond, Bond – the rest we can shoot like television.' John was an editor, then an action unit director before taking on the overall direction of the film. 'I have always valued my editing experience. It gives me the ability to look at an action sequence, then break it down into small segments for other people to film. I think that is my strength, being able to delegate and still come in on time. In some ways I'm a managing director,' he quipped.

On the set, John could be seen speeding up the action – condensing a line here, adding some pace to a movement there, continually refining the scene to keep it constantly moving.

When John took over the direction of the Bonds on *For Your Eyes Only*, everyone knew he would be extremely good at the action scenes but some people expressed initial reservations about his ability to work with actors. Those reservations have long gone. 'The stories, in a way, do not set out to be more than lightweight narratives. It's the development of character that is important.'

John is very pleased with this film because of the strength of the Sanchez character. He believes he is one of the strongest Bond villains and in Robert Davi's hands will be truly memorable. Casting the Bond women, on the other hand, can often be more difficult, since even today many actresses do not want to be in a Bond film. They feel it is exploitative. John agreed that this is not necessarily untrue. The women in the Bonds do still have decorative value. But in recent years they have striven to make the women's parts more important and more independent. Pam, in *Licence to Kill* is a good example.

'You have to prove yourself to the actors,' he commented. 'The Bond set is without pretence. It is very down-to-earth and there are no theatricals. It makes some of the actors uneasy because they aren't used to a situation where everyone knows what they're doing and goes about doing it quietly. Most are more accustomed to all sorts of screaming and shouting.' This is a direct result of the teamwork on the set.

'I think John has got an extraordinarily powerful sense of visual narrative and edits the film superbly,' Timothy Dalton said of his director. 'It gives you confidence that the film will be, without question, extremely well put together.'

Above: *Director John Glen discusses a point in the script with the new bond girl, Carey Lowell.*
Right: *Here John is showing Benicio del Toro, a young and charismatic henchman, how to wield his deadly knife.*

PROFILE

Name: John Glen

Bond history: *On Her Majesty's Secret Service* (editor, second unit director), *The Spy Who Loved Me* (editor, action unit director), *Moonraker* (editor, action unit director), *For Your Eyes Only* (director), *Octopussy* (director), *A View to a Kill* (director), *The Living Daylights* (director), *Licence to Kill* (director).

John Glen has the distinction of being the only person to direct five Bonds and since *For Your Eyes Only*, he has been the driving force behind the return to a thriller style. In the Bond annals, John will go down as the director who gave the Bond films their harder edge.

John started work in the industry as a messenger at Shepperton Studios near London under Alexander Korda. George Whitear, the stills photographer of the 2nd unit, was, incidentally, a contemporary in the same lowly position. In 1947, he began as a runner in the cutting-room. 'It was a different world in those days,' he recalled. 'You couldn't actually speak to the editor who worked in a room with the door shut. There was a hierarchy and a mystique about the whole process. It is much healthier today where young people can get opportunities earlier.'

John rose through the ranks, working as an assembly editor, a sound editor, and finally an editor, initially in television documentaries and then in television dramas. He recalled an early programme he edited in the 1960s, *Man of the World* for director Richard Green. 'He swore I'd ruined his film.' John began to direct action sequences for thrillers like TV's *Danger Man* and *Man With a Suitcase*, often doing some of the editing as well.

He was brought into the Bonds by Peter Hunt (they had previously been assistants together at Shepperton Studios) when Peter took over directing on *On Her Majesty's Secret Service*. Co-producers 'Cubby' Broccoli and Harry Saltzman were reluctant to use him, arguing that John was not experienced enough, having worked mainly in television. But John proved his worth directing the famous bob-run sequence in the film and they asked him to stay on. He directed the 2nd unit and edited the film.

John's favourite scene from a Bond movie and the one that established him forever as a master of action material is the pre-title 'parachute ski-jump' sequence of *The Spy Who Loved Me*. 'I spent $500,000 on that one jump – but it made an impact on my career.' In the meantime, apart from the Bonds, he was working with Euan Lloyd as an editor and action unit director on *The Wild Geese* (1978) and *The Sea Wolves* (1980). When 'Cubby' Broccoli was looking for a director after *Moonraker*, John found himself being taken to lunch and sized up. He was finally offered the chance to direct and has stayed, working full-time on the Bonds ever since.

19

LICENCE TO KILL

Right: *This production shot of the filming of the pre-title sequence shows one of the rigs used for manipulating Sanchez' plane. With this simple contraption, designed and made for* Licence to Kill, *the plane can be tilted at a variety of angles while filming takes place. It is especially important for close up work which can be cut into the main action.*

Right: *This excerpt from the storyboard details the action when Bond captures Sanchez' plane with the winch of his helicopter. As the surrounding stills show, the filmed scenes stay very close to the original storyboard – a necessity for this kind of action filming.*

PRE-TITLE SEQUENCE

The Bond films have justly become famous for their pre-title sequences. Action, humour and breathtaking stunts have combined to produce some memorable introductions to the main core of the films. *Licence to Kill* is no exception.

Bond and Felix Leiter, his long-standing friend and American colleague, are on their way to Leiter's wedding when they are diverted. A Drug Enforcement Administration (DEA) agent in a Coast Guard helicopter informs them that Sanchez,

a notorious drugs dealer, is in the area. Bond and Leiter, forgetting their personal commitments for the moment, give chase and an exciting sequence follows which climaxes in an unusual plane fight. Bond is lowered from the helicopter and 'captures' Sanchez' light aircraft like a spent fish on the end of a winch. The errant couple then head for the wedding and sky-dive down to the church, arriving in the nick of time.

Most of this action was filmed during the month that the crew

spent at Key West. Following the storyboard, the main unit, the second unit and a specially convened aerial unit each filmed sections of the sequence. Dovetailing the footage from the different units is a highly complex operation and the storyboard becomes the main guide.

Even a small part of the sequence – for example, the scene where Bond actually 'captures' the plane –involves numerous shots filmed in as many as three different ways: on the ground, in the air and in the studio. This method of shooting provides plenty of cover for the editor to compose the sequence, making it seem real, dangerous and exciting.

TAKE ONE

One morning, the second unit filmed Bond being lowered from the helicopter, grappling for a foothold on Sanchez' plane and putting the winch in place. Once edited, just this small section will contain about thirty cuts, moving between the footage shot by the second unit and that shot by the aerial crew. The second unit filmed the action from the ground which led to its own problems.

John Richardson and the special effects department had built a rig that allowed Sanchez' plane, a light Cessna, to be tipped at any angle from horizontal to vertical, simulating a nose-dive. A wind machine provided the equivalent of air currents and one of Ken Atherfold's special camera rigs allowed the camera to 'float', giving the impression of the scene being shot from the air. By Ken's standards, this rig was quite simple, relying on pieces of wood and stretchable 'bunjies' for its effect, but it is a good example of the kind of ingenuity that is always at work on the unit.

Timothy Dalton, watching the filming, was worried that the stuntman was not making the action look convincingly dangerous. 'I want to believe that there's a battle going on,' he explained. 'It should also have the feel of someone going fishing – you have to catch the plane on a hook.' Then Dalton took over and did the stunt himself, transforming it into something more exciting, emphasising the difference between an actor and a stuntman. 'It was fun,' he said later, recovering from having been lowered from a helicopter, on the end of a rope. 'It was just like flying. I was more worried when the plane was at full tilt. There was nothing to hold on to and the plane was moving around a lot when the helicopter was flying above it.'

Right: *Bond and Leiter are late because they have stopped off on the way to capture a dangerous criminal.*

Below: *The wedding party awaits the late arrival of Felix Leiter and his best man, James Bond – they 'drop in' by the shortest route.*

Above: *Felix Leiter (David Hedison) and his best man, James Bond, arrive in spectacular style for the wedding.*

Nevertheless, the sky-dive part of the sequence went ahead on schedule. The helicopter was circling some 900m (3000 ft) above the target so that the sky-dive would take five minutes. After two minutes everyone took up their positions by the two cameras and waited. Gradually the dots in the sky took on the shape of the sky-divers. They hit the target, outside the church, exactly on the first attempt but did not manage to land beside each other as they had intended –the wind had blown them apart. The camera operators, however, were happy with what they had captured and it was agreed not to do it again. The stunt had worked first time.

B.J. WORTH

B.J. Worth is the parachute stunt co-ordinator on *Licence to Kill*. He has worked on most of the Bonds since *Moonraker*, when he did the pre-title stunt where Bond is thrown out of a plane without a parachute. He has done so many aerial stunts subsequently that his young son slept through the spectacular jump from the Eiffel Tower (in *A View to a Kill*), totally disinterested.

B.J. who has made award-winning films about sky-diving, was captain of the team that won the World Sky-Diving Championship on three consecutive occasions. Now he has his own sky-diving company which, amongst other things, did the jump at the opening ceremony of the Seoul Olympics. They had worked on it for over two years, planning and practising how to form the five Olympic rings in the air with 96 jumpers.

Each jump is different. '*Moonraker* was interesting,' he recalled, 'because it showed the action from an angle that the audience rarely sees. The hardest part was having the cameraman in free fall at the same time.'

'A stunt like today's is totally unnerving,' he admitted 'as there are no alternative landing spots.' Because of the winds, they had to make a different approach from the one they had planned but it worked out to everyone's satisfaction. 'We give them what they want – usually on the first take,' he boasted.

TAKE TWO

On another day, the main unit filmed outside the church. Della, the bride, is waiting anxiously for Leiter to arrive. The helicopter flies above them with Sanchez' plane in tow, while Leiter, the groom, and Bond, the best man, parachute down to the wedding.

The Federal Aviation Administration (FAA) decreed that if the helicopter were going to fly with the lightweight plane winched beneath it, then the whole of the flight path had to be cleared for safety reasons. The production department had already had to inconvenience local people by turning off the electricity in the area (to avoid the parachutes getting entangled with power lines) and closing some of the roads to allow filming to take place. They thought that clearing the flight path too might cause a lot of resentment, so they decided against filming the whole sequence at Key West and looked for alternatives.

Above left: *John Glen watches while Paul Weston demonstrates a stunt to Timothy Dalton which involves a tank of maggots.* **Above right:** *John show Timothy the camera angle for the next shot.* **Below:** *The water-skiing sequence is one of the most unusual in the film.*

When doubling for Jaws, Paul Weston realized his lack of metallic teeth gave him away. So he covered a crescent of orange peel with silver paper from a cigarette packet. When they asked if he was ready for action, he could not answer with all that in his mouth.

THE STUNTS

Whenever there is a stunt – on land, sea or in the air, on skis or with parachutes – on the Bond film, Paul Weston is the man who finds the people who can do it and then co-ordinates the action, working out how best to achieve what is in the script. He can be seen on the set, walking through the action, counting and practising with his team of stunt-men to react as if they had struck a reef, jumped into the water to escape an out-of-control boat about to hit a jetty, pulled punches, taken tumbles or fallen off buildings.

Paul is the first to admit that he 'loves playing with big toys' and he relishes scenes like the desert battle in *The Living Daylights* where he had 64 horsemen, explosions, trucks and tanks. 'A big scene like that takes a lot of organizing,' he commented.

'You have to co-ordinate the action in a practical as well as a spectacular way,' he explained. 'It has to be physically possible and done for the right price in the right location. It is more of a technical job –casting the right people with the right ability and adhering to the storyboards. The writers have an idea of what should happen and it's up to us to make it work.' On *Licence to Kill*, his team of stuntmen included parachutists, underwater experts,

drivers and specialized water-skiers.

Paul obviously has great respect for Timothy Dalton and what he has to do to play Bond. 'We got on very well from the first four minutes of the last Bond. We looked at each other as he was coming down the rock on the top of the jeep in the pre-title sequence in Gibraltar. I could have wired him on to the jeep so that he could not move and we would have got the shot. I told

him, "You've got four minutes to prove that you're Bond." He said, "Exactly." It was a straight run but it took courage to be on the top. He did it and did it very well.'

'If it's a bit hairy for Timothy, but it's quite safe, then it's up to his courage.' Paul went on to talk about the scene in *Licence to Kill* where Bond is lowered from a helicopter. 'A lot of actors would not do it. That's where Timothy is playing Bond, like no one ever before.'

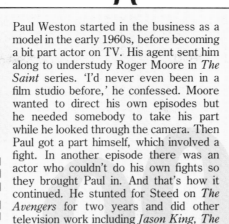

PROFILE

Name: Paul Weston

Bond history: *The Man With the Golden Gun* (stuntman), *The Spy Who Loved Me* (stuntman), *Moonraker* (stuntman), *Octopussy* (stunt supervisor), *The Living Daylights* (action sequences supervisor), *Licence to Kill* (action sequences supervisor).

Paul Weston started in the business as a model in the early 1960s, before becoming a bit part actor on TV. His agent sent him along to understudy Roger Moore in *The Saint* series. 'I'd never even been in a film studio before,' he confessed. Moore wanted to direct his own episodes but he needed somebody to take his part while he looked through the camera. Then Paul got a part himself, which involved a fight. In another episode there was an actor who couldn't do his own fights so they brought Paul in. And that's how it continued. He stunted for Steed on *The Avengers* for two years and did other television work including *Jason King, The Adventurers* and *The Protectors*.

Simon Crane, the stunt co-ordinator of the second unit is a younger, newer recruit to the field. He had to qualify to instructor level in six different sports and undertake a five year apprenticeship *and* obtain an equity card before he could practise. Paul comes from an earlier tradition. 'Getting the job was the biggest

stunt,' he recalled. 'We learned as we went along. We had no help from anyone, as people were protecting their own jobs. You had to be careful, keep your eyes open, your mouth shut and listen to what was going on.'

Paul has worked on several Bonds as a stunt performer, beginning with *The Man With the Golden Gun*. He has taken part in fights and explosions, fallen off the gantry in *The Spy Who Loved Me* in the submarine scene and many other stunts. He doubled for Jaws on *Moonraker* in which he made the daring jump from one cable car to another in Rio de Janeiro, leaping about 5m (15 ft) across to a mini-trampoline on top of the second car. He also jumped cars on a motorcycle, Evil Knievel style, for a live television show.

Nowadays he is much in demand, working on action films like the *Superman* series, directing his own TV movie *Gulag*, dabbling in lyric writing and, of course, working on the Bonds.

Left: *Bond indulges in a spot of climbing in order to observe what is happening in Sanchez' office. He has abseiled down from the roof of the building.*

Right: *Among the hazards of Milton Krest's laboratory for the unwary visitor is this tank and its 'electric' occupant.*

Paul Weston has suffered several injuries while stunting. During a parachute fall in *A Bridge Too Far* (1977) he smashed his ankles. While flying in *Superman* (1978), the wires broke and he fell on his head from about 5m (15 ft), breaking his cheekbone and damaging his wrists and knees. While making *The Return of the Jedi* (1983), a wire broke and he fell about 6m (20 ft) down an embankment. Someone fell on top of him and he broke his leg.

Paul Weston tells a story about one incident. He was looking forward to one particular stunt – climbing a high building – and desperate to get on with the action. The first assistant said to him, 'Hold on a minute. Who are you doing this for' and, Paul admitted, 'He was quite right. I should have been thinking more about the movie. It was a good lesson for me.'

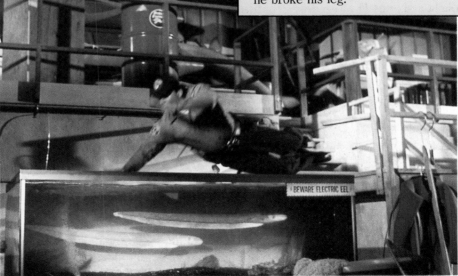

FELIX LEITER AND THE WEDDING

Bond's long-standing American friend, Felix Leiter, returns to the fray in *Licence to Kill*. Indeed the film opens on Leiter's wedding day: he is marrying a headstrong Southern belle, named Della. Bond, a close friend of both bride and groom, is best man. It is Bond who, after a hectic diversion, delivers Leiter to the church, Bond who receives Della's wedding garter (indicating the next person to get married) and Bond who is given a cigarette lighter by the happy couple as a token of their friendship.

Leiter has been on the track of Sanchez for some years and – with Bond – is largely responsible for his capture. When Sanchez escapes, therefore, he vents his spleen on Leiter. Bond finds his friend in a mangled condition ('he disagreed with something that ate him') and seeks his own revenge getting his 'licence to kill' removed in the process. It is the firm friendship between the two men, central to the film's story, which leads to Bond's action as an independent.

Right: *Felix Leiter (David Hedison) is tied up with a problem – a shark snapping away hungrily at his heels. It is Sanchez' revenge for his earlier capture.*

Opposite page: *Leiter survives and ends up in hospital. His visitors – Bond and Sharkey (Frank McRae) – are determined to carry on where Leiter left off.*

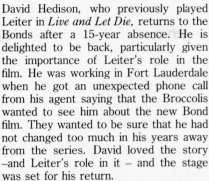

PROFILE

Name: David Hedison

Alias: Felix Leiter
Job description: CIA agent
Bond history: *Live and Let Die*, *Licence to Kill*.

David Hedison, who previously played Leiter in *Live and Let Die*, returns to the Bonds after a 15-year absence. He is delighted to be back, particularly given the importance of Leiter's role in the film. He was working in Fort Lauderdale when he got an unexpected phone call from his agent saying that the Broccolis wanted to see him about the new Bond film. They wanted to be sure that he had not changed too much in his years away from the series. David loved the story –and Leiter's role in it – and the stage was set for his return.

'I feel as though I've picked up where I left off, although I feel different playing it with Timothy from how I did with Roger. They are complete opposites. Roger never takes anything seriously. I think that's why he is so funny. Timothy is very earnest. He takes his work very seriously, cares about the scene and works very well with his fellow actor, bending over backwards to help him.'

David, a native of Rhode Island, trained in New York at the Neighbourhood Playhouse in the same class as people like Steve McQueen and Joanne Woodward. His first real break in the theatre came with his performance in *A Month in the Country* starring Uta Hagen and directed by Sir Michael Redgrave. Some talent scouts saw it, he had a screen test and ended up under contract to Fox.

'In that time I did a lot of forgettable films,' he recalled. After the submarine adventure, *The Enemy Below* (1957), he got his first starring role as *The Fly* (1958) with Vincent Price. An earlier series, *Five Fingers*, led to a change of name. Until then, he had been known as Al Hedison but the network felt this was not very romantic and wanted something more suave. So he used his middle name and became David Hedison. (His real name is, in fact, Ara Heditsian.)

He is, perhaps, best-known for his role in the long-running TV series, *Voyage to the Bottom of the Sea*. 'I recently got a very interesting letter from a fan asking if I was related to Al Hedison as we looked very much alike, although she thought that I was slightly better looking,' he said with a chuckle.

David was living in London when Tom Mankiewicz, a close friend who had just written the script for *Live and Let Die*, saw him in *Summer and Smoke* (1961), and thought he might make a good Felix Leiter. In the event, he was cast even before it was decided who would be the new Bond. More recently, he has been working in Britain and America on adventure films like *The Naked Face* (1985) and *North Sea Hijack* (1979), both of which starred Roger Moore. His return to the series marks the first time that Leiter has been played by the same person.

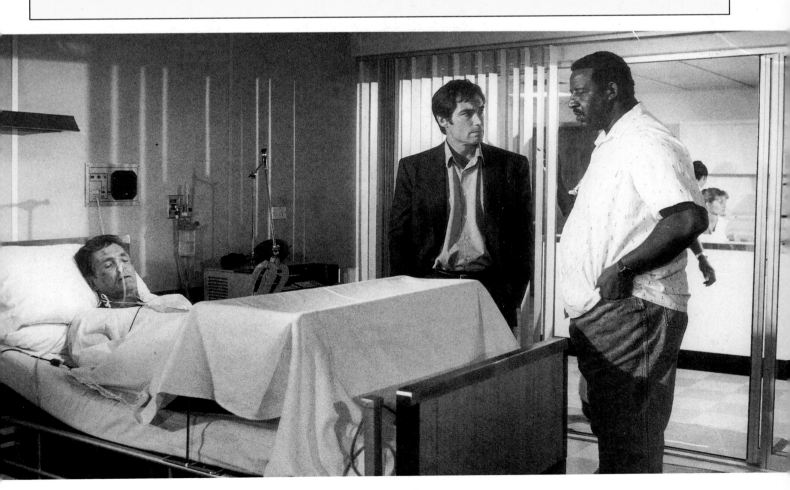

THE WEDDING

All the glamour and style of the Bonds is in evidence in the wedding sequence: the marriage ceremony and the reception. Large crowds, lavish costumes and lush sets provide the background for Leiter's marriage to Della while the spectacular last-minute descent to the church by the groom and best man adds to the excitement.

Extras from all over Key West were brought in to appear as wedding guests. This gave Jodie Tillen, the costume designer, a major problem as most people on the island habitually wear T-shirts and jeans. So she went on a rapid shopping spree to New York with Barbara Broccoli, buying up model dresses and samples from the fashion houses, in order to give the scene its glittering feel.

Della's wedding dress, made of re-embroidered French lace adorned with seed pearls and opal sequins, is an original. Because of the vagaries of the filming process – the scene where Della is attacked was filmed before the wedding sequence – two dresses had to be made. This meant locating 17m (18 yds) of very expensive material. (It cost $150 a metre). No one shop stocked a lot of it so lengths had to be collected from different places around the States. Panic broke out for two long days in the costume department when they were still short of three metres. Della's bridal car is a white Lincoln limousine.

The wedding reception was filmed in Key West in the delightful gardens of the home of interior designer, Stefano Marchetti. Since 1979, when he bought the house, he has gradually landscaped its gardens using papaya, banana palms, hibiscus, spiky sago palms, pondorosa lemon and other tropical vegetation, setting the plants off with Sicilian jars and Tuscan pots. It makes an attractive setting for the reception, capturing the exotic flavour of Key West. Stefano was delighted with the film crew –who painted parts of the house that were becoming a little shabby – and is looking forward to people hiring his gardens so as to have their reception in the place where the Bond film was shot.

The wedding cake was baked by the chef of the Casa Marina, the hotel where many of the unit stayed. A white cake with raspberry filling, it had to be an exact match of the one used for the interior scenes, shot in Mexico, even down to its gold trim and royal icing lace fringe which had to be added at the last minute to keep it fresh.

When it was time for Della and Leiter to serve the cake to their guests, all sorts of confusion ensued when the director said 'cut'.

Above: *David Hedison, Priscilla Barnes and Timothy Dalton share a joke while a shot of the wedding reception is prepared.*

When in harness for the sky-dive down to his wedding scene, David Hedison had a minor accident. The harness was supposed to shoot him out at a certain level and it went wrong. 'I went splat on the cement – feet first – and the shock went from my toes right up to my waist. My first thoughts were, "Oh, my god, I've broken both my legs." I was really frightened. But then I got up and walked around and everything was fine.'

Below: *Leiter has serious business with Bond, even on his wedding day.*
Opposite page: *Della and Leiter cut the cake, but what should be a happy day is soon turned to tragedy.*

One of the wedding guests, Sandi Sentell, had won a competition to get her part. MTV and VH1 ran a televised appeal advertising that 'you could be the next Bond girl'. Over 20,000 people sent in their photographs. Eight of which were short-listed and interviewed over the telephone and, finally, Sandi was offered the chance.

She is a former all-American cheerleader from the University of Tennessee who is now a dance and gymnastics teacher in Atlanta, Georgia. Her father is an avid Bond fan and her family came with her for her big scene. 'It's exciting and real fun,' she commented. After the film, Sandi can look forward to a lot of publicity – appearances on *The Johnny Carson Show* and articles in Cosmopolitan were mentioned.

The wedding sequence called for a wedding photographer to be in shot – and none of the extras were suitable. Keith Hamshere, the unit's stills photographer came to the rescue and found himself, for once, in front of the cameras. Acting is not, however, totally foreign to Keith as he was in fact the first *Oliver* on the London stage.

PRISCILLA BARNES

Leiter's bride, Della, is played by kookie New Jersey blonde Priscilla Barnes. With an early ambition to be a Rockette, her career in show business began with modelling and beauty contests – she won the Miss Hollywood title. She landed a part in a Bob Hope USO Christmas Show but her dancing career was abruptly ended when she fell off-stage during a performance and broke a leg.

A chance meeting with Peter Falk and a part in *Colombo* led her into acting. Her films include *The Last Married Couple in America* (1979) and *Sunday Lovers* (1980) but she is probably best-known for her role as the 'dumb blonde' character in the US version of television's *Three's Company*.

Another of the extras at the wedding was Doug Redenius, a post-man from Chicago, Illinois. He has a large, private collection of Bond memorabilia, comprising over 1800 items ranging from costumes and props to marketed items such as a James Bond road-race set, complete with tracks, tunnels and a model Aston Martin.

THE ASSIGNMENT

Licence to Kill makes a crucial break from previous Bond films in that there is no formal assignment. When Della and Leiter, Bond's long-time friend, are brutally assaulted on their wedding day, Bond is set on revenge. But M, not convinced by this course of action, tries to dissuade 007 from his mission. In the ensuing row, M revokes Bond's licence to kill and, for the first time, Bond embarks on an operation as an individual.

Tracking down Leiter's assailants brings Bond into contact with Franz Sanchez, a notorious underworld villain whose drug-dealing activities support a powerful Latin American empire. On Leiter's wedding day, he and Bond interrupt the nuptials to capture Sanchez but with the aid of a corrupt DEA agent, the drug baron later escapes. Pam Bouvier, a freelance associate of Leiter is contacted by Bond as a possible ally. She and Bond join forces, albeit with deep mutual suspicion. Meanwhile Moneypenny, seriously worried about leaving Bond on his own, sends Q into the field to assist.

Above: *When Bond finds Leiter the worse for his encounter with the shark, he is visibly upset. It is this long-standing friendship between the two allies that fuels the rest of the story.*

Above right: *Pam, played by Carey Lowell, demonstrates the hidden talents of the Polaroid camera.*

Right: *The signature gun has been designed to be quickly fitted together from seemingly innocuous camera parts*

Pam, Q and 007 pit their wits against Sanchez and his hand-picked team at their headquarters in Isthmus City and try to bring the villain to justice.

EQUIPMENT ISSUED

Just when Bond thinks he is firmly on his own on this assignment, he returns to his hotel to find that his 'uncle' has arrived. This improbable character turns out to be Q (Desmond Llewellyn), dressed in Bermuda shorts and looking very much the stylish holiday-maker.

Q's suitcase contains all the equipment necessary for a field operative but cunningly designed as common-place pieces of tourist gear. He hands Bond a travel alarm clock neatly packed with explosives; a standard British passport which detonates on opening; a Hasselblad camera which can be broken apart and reconstructed as a gun; a Polaroid camera which shoots out laser beams and takes X-ray pictures; and yet more explosive, disguised as toothpaste.

THE SIGNATURE GUN

The Camera that becomes a weapon

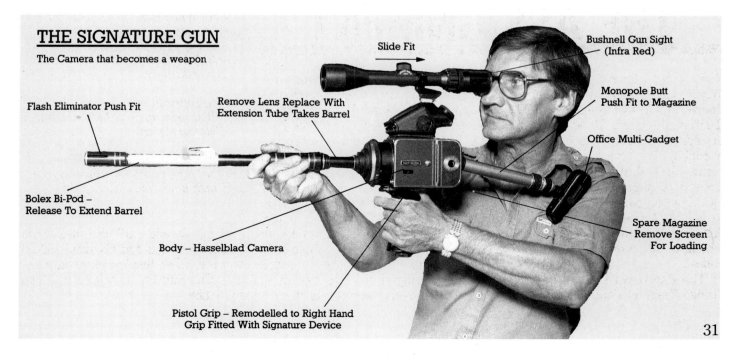

Slide Fit

Bushnell Gun Sight (Infra Red)

Monopole Butt Push Fit to Magazine

Office Multi-Gadget

Flash Eliminator Push Fit

Remove Lens Replace With Extension Tube Takes Barrel

Bolex Bi-Pod – Release To Extend Barrel

Body – Hasselblad Camera

Spare Magazine Remove Screen For Loading

Pistol Grip – Remodelled to Right Hand Grip Fitted With Signature Device

31

The 'signature gun', the one that packs away to look like a camera, is computerized for a personal user by means of an optical palm reader so it may be fired by one individual only. It is still in its experimental stages but Q has managed to smuggle one out for Bond's use.

Desmond Llewelyn, who has played Q in every Bond film since *From Russia With Love*, recalled that the man who designed the memorable briefcase in that film also had a hand in designing the signature gun. Following the script suggestion that the gun should be constructed from something that Q could be carrying innocently, without arousing suspicion, Peter Lamont and the art department bought a range of different cameras for the special effects boys who laid them all out on a table and tried to see how a gun could be made to resemble a camera. They found the Hasselblad camera with Bushnell gun sight components the most suitable for their needs. Gradually the concept developed into a gun and the engineers then made the parts so that they fitted together.

Right: *Bond carrying the signature gun looks as dangerous as the hardware.*
Below: *007 goes into action with an unusual partner, Q, played as always by Desmond Llewelyn.*

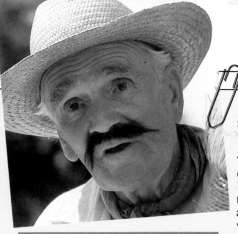

PROFILE

Name: Desmond Llewelyn

Alias: Q

Job description: to develop new equipment for the double-0 agents

Bond history: *From Russia With Love, Goldfinger, Thunderball, You Only Live Twice, On Her Majesty's Secret Service, Diamonds Are Forever, The Man With the Golden Gun, The Spy Who Loved Me, Moonraker, For Your Eyes Only, Octopussy, A View to a Kill, The Living Daylights, Licence to Kill*

Desmond Llewelyn, relishing one of the few location trips that his many years' association with the Bond films has brought, talked about how Q got his character.

'If it weren't for Guy Hamilton I would never have thought of playing Q this way,' he confessed. On *From Russia With Love*, the first Bond he did with Terence Young in the director's chair (they had also worked together on *They Were Not Divided*, 1951), they discussed the part. Young wanted him to play Q as a Welsh ex-sergeant-major type but Llewelyn wanted him to be an English civil servant. Then, in *Goldfinger* (directed by Hamilton), Q is fiddling at his bench when Bond comes in. Hamilton interrupted the filming, saying Desmond had got it all wrong, 'You can't stand this man.' 'From that moment on,' recalled Desmond, "I played him with that slight antagonism –'I never joke about my work, 007." I would have played him more as an eager-beaver. In the end he is the only person who treats Bond with contempt.'

'Q is a unique part,' he continued, 'because I'm treated like a general on a private's pay. I may only have one scene so I'm not going to get a fortune. But everyone knows me. I've even been called a living legend and it's great to be appreciated and recognized – after all, one is an actor, an egotist.'

Desmond is a lovely down-to-earth man, given to spates of self-mockery, but who can show sudden passions for all sorts of things. He lectures to children for charity and is a mine of information about the Bond gadgets. His favourite is still the Aston Martin (in *Goldfinger*) with its ejector seat. 'What is so brilliant about the gadgets,' he enthused, 'is that there is nothing new. Take the car. Knives coming out of the wheels were seen with Boedicea and Ben Hur; the ejector seat comes from airplanes; oil slicks were used in *G-Men* (1935) and so on. But the cleverness is putting all that together in one vehicle.' He went on to remind me that the homing device used in *Goldfinger* was invented by the Royal Navy.

He remarked with irony that he, himself, is not very good with technical equipment, 'I just have to touch any gadget and it goes wrong.' Cash dispenser cards, digital watches, computer games are all doomed in his hands. But people who see the Bond films cannot believe this and he often suffers comments like, 'I would have thought you'd know how to fix it.'

Desmond talks with passion about the cinema and the need to see films on the big screen. There is a scene in *Octopussy* where Q walks across the action. On TV he does it for no apparent reason but in the cinema you can see that he is working on a car on the side of the frame. The significance is lost on television. 'You must make a point of saying that in your book,' he emphasized.

Desmond Llewelyn first went on location in *Thunderball*. A scene originally scheduled for Pinewood was moved to the Bahamas. 'I was wet weather cover,' he explained. 'I spent three or four weeks hanging around and I wasn't allowed to get sunburnt.' One day, when it seemed obvious that it was never going to rain, they decided to send him home and do the scene in England. As Desmond went for his last swim, it started raining. They cancelled the flight.

Below: *In this film, Q is one traveller who is prepared for any emergency. His suitcase is packed with typically Bondish gadgets, designed for use in tight situations, but disguised as ordinary pieces of luggage.*

Licence to Kill is one Bond film where Q actually joins in the action, taking on parts of the assignment, handling cars and boats, wearing disguises and generally becoming an assistant to Bond. This is one of the most attractive aspects of the script as Q has long been a great favourite with audiences.

Desmond Llewelyn is very pleased with this script and his more active part. 'Roger, I adore –I think he's one of the finest technical actors. He was brilliant the way he took over from Sean – and it was all the more difficult because he was *The Saint*. Now, with Timothy, we've got a real character – he's a thinking Bond, very modern. This is the first time we've ever seen an unshaven Bond – which he would be when he's been in a fight.'

In *Thunderball*, Desmond Llewelyn loved the scene where he was demonstrating the underwater camera to Bond. 'I had lovely lines like, "Pay attention, 007," and Bond was acting like a schoolboy.' Peter Hunt, who edited the film, had to cut around the scene using shots that were got before and after the take itself. 'They were the best notices I've ever had in a Bond and I wasn't even acting.'

GUNS AND THE ARMOURER

As in all James Bond films, there are guns everywhere: small pistols, sub-machine guns, rifles and even a sawn-off shotgun. Whenever Bond escapes from a tricky situation or tackles a villain, there are always guns and the right gun has to be used at the right time for the action to look realistic.

The guns in *Licence to Kill* are supplied and supervised by Stembridge Gun Rentals Inc, a company which boasts of having Cecil B. De-Mille as one of their first customers – they have been working with the film industry since 1921. Harris R. Bierman, one of three different Stembridge employees on the film, spent 13 years in the LA County Sheriff's Department before entering the gun retail trade and, later, finding a place in the movies. He looks like a caricature of a Canadian Mountie, complete with a neat moustache. He speaks in a slow, measured drawl, clearly familiar with every intricate detail of each gun he supplies. He was able to talk about all the firearms in this film.

Bond, of course, carries his traditional Walther PPK but he is unarmed when en route to Felix Leiter's wedding, so in the opening helicopter sequence a DEA agent gives him a Brazilian copy of the Beretta (Bond's original gun in the Fleming novels which is taken away in *Thunderball*) – the Taurus PT-99 – to fend off the bad guys. The Taurus is a 9mm Parabellum calibre gun which typically carries 16 rounds. It is heavier and altogether more powerful than the Walther PPK and not nearly so compact.

Pam has a Beretta 950, a 25 automatic (known as the Jetfire). It is deadly at close range though its sights are rudimentary. 'It's basically what we call in the States a 'belly gun', Harris explained. 'Even so, a properly placed bullet or a fusillade of bullets would probably cause the victim to perish.' It is meant to be carried in a very small area like a back pocket or a handbag and is used for very close range encounters when a larger gun cannot be employed. Pam gets involved in some pretty tight situations in the film where a small pistol like this is most effective.

Pam has a nickel-plated version which, according to Harris, is 'quite flashy'. A woman's gun, it nestles nicely in the hand and, in the film, is made to fit into a special lace garter cum leg-holster, developed by Jodie Tillen, the costume designer. Harris had trouble getting enough of these pistols on time because the Beretta factory in Maryland only makes one run of the nickel-plated versions a year.

Harris had one difficult request on this film – for a Mossberg 'Rogue' gun. This is the shotgun that Pam uses to blow a hole in the Barrelhead Bar when she and Bond are trying to escape. 'When the Mossberg people in the United States heard it was being used in a Bond film, they immediately sent us out four samples to get them on the film quickly,' Harris said.

The Micro-Mini Uzi sub-machine gun features prominently in the film, particularly in the climactic tanker chase. It has a 9mm Parabellum calibre which fires 32 rounds, very similar to the Taurus. This small machine

Carey Lowell demonstrates the Mossberg Rouge gun which Pam Carey uses to blow a hole in the wall of the Barrelhead Bar. The hole is big enough for Pam and Bond to crawl through to safety.

gun has quite a fast firing action but it is small enough to be carried like a relatively large-size hand-gun which, according to Harris, is a deadly combination. 'We've just done a scene with it, at Key West, where one of the bad guys at the bar tries to stop Pam and Bond escaping into the cigarette boat. The villain is carrying the Uzi. Due to Bond's incredible luck, the rear end of the boat gets hit, Bond miraculously survives and one shot from his Walther downs this denizen. Of course, this is what makes a Bond picture what it is.'

Finally, Harris added a note for the British viewers of this film – the M16 A1, carried by Sanchez' guards, was used by the SAS in the invasion of the Falklands. 'It's somewhat familiar to Her Majesty's forces,' he commented 'and well respected by them, I'm sure.'

> When automatic pistols are converted to fire blanks on films, they cannot be reconverted to fire live ammunition again. A lot of metal has to be taken out of the locking surfaces, the slide and the barrel to enable the pistols to function properly with blanks.

SAFETY PRECAUTIONS

The armourer's other responsibility on a film set is the safety of the actors and the crew. Special precautions have to be taken even when firing blanks because they too can be dangerous in very close shots. The camera is surrounded by a large shield of perspex (plexiglass) and the camera crew are covered by heavy blankets. Whenever a gun is fired close to the crew or camera, the armourer makes sure that the angles are such that nobody is fired at directly. Live ammunition is never used. In the case of large charges, 'we cheat,' as Harris put it. 'We ask the actors and the crew to stay far enough apart to ensure that safety rules are constantly observed.'

The issuing of the weapons to extras and actors is strictly controlled. After each set is finished and the guns have been fired, the armourer will immediately come up to the actors and take control of the arms, making sure they are unloaded and in a safe condition until they are needed once again. 'We never allow an actor or an extra to take a weapon off the set,' Harris explained. 'Or to take blank amunition with them.

We control everything that has to do with firearms and blank ammunition on the film. That way we have no worries.'

Some directors, as Harris knows only too well, get a little too gung-ho and he has to step in and say, 'No, that is not going to be safe.' But he has no such worries on a Bond film. 'Everybody here is really careful. They're a professional bunch of folks. It's a very enjoyable set. They've done this for a long time and they know what they're doing and I'm very confident with them.'

Below: *Bond has his victim within his sights.* **Bottom:** *Robert Davi displays the whole range of guns used in the film. Each one has been chosen for its authenticity in a particular situation.*

ENEMY PERSONNEL

SANCHEZ

Sanchez may not be the most terrifying of Bond's opponents, but he is certainly the most lifelike. He is a villain plucked straight from today's headlines a Latin American drug lord whose wealth buys him power. If he does not like what a newspaper writes, he can buy out the newspaper; if he does not like the policies of a particular government, he can buy the President.

Sanchez is dangerous and ambitious, aiming to extend his empire to the Far East and, eventually, the world. He is a man of great charm and humour – but is also capable of authorizing extreme acts of violence. Like the new, more realistic James Bond, he is a contemporary character, far removed from 007's caricatured opponents of the Seventies.

Robert Davi, who plays Sanchez, argues he is the first villain to make James Bond compromise his professionalism and become emotionally involved in his self-imposed assignment. It is a conflict which gives a great deal of added bite to the drama being played out between the two main protagonists.

There is a classic Bond scene, typical of the early Connery movies, when Sanchez assembles a group of Oriental businessmen in his office who are potential colleagues and reveals his master plan: to set up an invisible power empire from Chile to the Pacific. One of them, Kwang, distrusts the set-up and challenges Sanchez, only to find himself on the receiving end of Sanchez' far-reaching power.

Although Sanchez has a host of henchmen to carry out his orders, when he goes into action himself he can be dangerous.
Left: *Sanchez is seen here with the Captain of his Guard, Heller (played by Don Stroud), disposing of a troublesome intruder.*
Below: *When Braun (Guy de St Cyr) has Bond in his grasp, Sanchez has no hesitation in telling him what he can do with 007.*

Left: *When his hideaway is invaded by the Drug Enforcement Agency, Sanchez tries to escape. On this occasion, Leiter's wedding day, he is caught but he later escapes to do battle with James Bond another day.*

37

PROFILE

Name: Robert Davi

Alias: Franz Sanchez
Job description: drug-runner
Bond history: *Licence to Kill*

Robert Davi, who was born in Astoria, New York, began acting at school, but entered the entertainment world initially as an opera singer. He studied under Tito Gobbi and made his debut with the Lyric Opera Company when he was 19.

On graduating from high-school he won a drama scholarship to Hofstra University, where they had a replica of the Globe stage and an annual Shakespearian festival. Here Robert could indulge his love of Shakespeare while receiving a classical theatrical training. He later went to Manhattan and studied with Stella Adler at the famous Actors' Studio.

His first film was a Movie of The Week – *Contract on Cherry Street* – starring Frank Sinatra, in which he played a Greek underworld figure. It began a career for him of villains and hoods. He has played a mercenary (in Arnold Schwarzenegger's *Raw Deal*, 1986), a Mafioso (in *The Gangster Chronicles*, 1981) and an undercover vice cop (in occasional episodes of *Hill Street Blues*). But his most important role to date was in the three-hour CBS production of *Terrorist on Trial – the US vs Salim Ajami* (1988) co-starring Sam Waterston and Ron Liebman. 'It is not an action but an intellectual piece,' he told me. 'It is a courtroom drama. I play a Palestinian, kidnapped by the US government to stand trial for acts of terrorism. I immersed myself in the part and did a lot of research.' It was a great critical success, especially for Robert.

He is a long-standing aquaintance of Tina Banta (one of 'Cubby' Broccoli's daughters). When *Terrorist on Trial* was on television, she deliberately did not call her father's attention to it, aware that he rarely responds to that kind of pressure. 'Cubby' caught it anyway. When it had finished, co-author Richard Maibaum phoned up excitedly to say, 'That's our guy,' 'Cubby' agreed; Robert was cast.

'It was a dream,' he said. 'When I was a kid, you were always affected the moment you heard the Bond theme song, wanting to be involved in that fantasy world. Getting the part is like becoming part of film history.

'Sanchez is a man who wants power – political, sexual and financial power – he combines them all,' Robert continued, talking about his role. 'He expects total loyalty from his underlings. Every character has a battle between light and dark within him, and Sanchez has to be very formidable, very real to stand up to Bond.'

He researched the part, reading factual books about the Latin American drug lords, searching out newspaper clippings and magazine articles and finally meeting people from that part of the world who have dealings with the narcotics underworld.

'His power is threatening,' Robert explained, 'because drugs are only a means. He also has an ideological aim: domination of the world.'

Right: *Anthony Zerbe plays Milton Krest, Sanchez' frontman in the drug-running trade.*
Below: *He meets an explosive end when he is trapped – with loads of Sanchez' money – in a decompression chamber. The money comes out of the encounter safe, if dirty.*

MILTON KREST

Milton Krest is a key member of Sanchez' organization. His headquarters are aboard the research vessel, *Wavekrest*. Apparently involved in a research project, breeding geneti-

Left: *Truman-Lodge (Anthony Starke) explains his complex financial and marketing strategy for improved sales to Sanchez' potential colleagues in the Far East.*
Below: *The same office, Sanchez' inner sanctum, after Bond has lit the fuse.*

cally engineered fish to solve the problems of hunger in the Third World, the *Wavekrest* is really the distribution base for Sanchez' drug-running operation. Krest is in fact a character taken directly from Ian Fleming's short story *The Hildebrand Rarity* and provided the initial inspiration for the story of the film.

Krest, once a formidable man, is often rather the worse for alcohol and is now merely a puppet for Sanchez' plans. A pathetic, almost ridiculous figure, he meets an explosive end in a decompression chamber.

Krest is played by the distinguished stage actor, Anthony Zerbe, who is also well-known to television viewers as a bad guy in series like *Mission Impossible*, *Bonanza* and *Gun Story*. He has an impressive theatrical record ranging from Broadway to the Canadian Shakespeare Festival. On film, as he put it, 'I've worked with some of the best – John Wayne, Katharine Hepburn, Steve McQueen.'

Anthony, who trained at the Stella Adler theatre school in New York, is an erudite man, eager to discuss the state of the American theatre, philosophy, poetry and the theory of acting.

He sees Krest as essentially a reactive part – like many fictional villains and he somewhat mockingly compares Krest to Iago. 'I try to centre the man in terms of things going on around him. He never really has a very happy moment in the film. From the first appearance of Bond, things go from bad to worse so we are not seeing a man at the height of his powers. We are seeing somebody buffeted by the slings and arrows of Mr Bond. He's a necessary cliché.'

'I became a villain because of my eyebrows and my name. If I'd been called Herbie Zerbe, I'd have been a comedian. I couldn't resist the offer because I'm so often a villain and this is the ultimate villain's movie.

'Besides,' he continued, 'I justify the best line in the movie.' When he meets his gruesome demise, blood and guts land everywhere, all over Sanchez' money. Sanchez calmly turns to an assistant. 'Launder it!' he commands.

39

THE WAVEKREST

In real life, the *Wavekrest* is the research vessel *J.W. Powell*, captained by Joe Newhouse. It is a part of the Perry Oceanographics organization. For two weeks it became the centre for filming in Key West.

Mr Pery, who heads the organization, is a forerunner in the development of ocean submersibles. Always trying to break new ground, his latest project is to extract fuel from sea water. Perry Oceanographics, itself, sounds like an organization invented for a Bond film. They have an island set-up in the Bahamas, Lee Stocking Island, which is staffed exclusively by scientific personnel – geologists, biologists and so on. They are currently taking freshwater fish from Africa and trying to get them to adapt to salt water as an inexpensive source of food for the Third World – just like Milton Krest's cover story.

The *J.W. Powell* conducts various kinds of oceanographic work. It was built in the Gulf of Mexico and originally used as a supply boat supporting the oil industry. The US Government took it over and did extensive work to it, turning it into a fully-equipped research vessel.

Nowadays it has all the equipment necessary to support detailed research projects when it is chartered by universities or the US Navy. It can supply small support boats, certified diving operators, remote control vehicles, submersibles, side-scan sonar, magnetometers, a decompression chamber, very specialized navigational equipment and biological sampling equipment. It has three laboratories on board – two of which are dry and one is under water. It can also support off-shore construction.

The ship can take on a range of projects. A recent one involved studying how the plates of the earth are shifting to form mountains, where land masses once were and where continents are going.

Perry's relationship with James Bond began on *The Spy Who Loved Me* and the development of the submersible car which provides some of the film's most exciting – and humorous – scenes. Ken Adam, then the production designer, outlined what he wanted using the Lotus Esprit as a model. Lotus supplied three bodies which were slightly sub-standard and then Perry got involved, testing their performance in the water and satisfying themselves that Ken's notion could work. In the end, there were, in fact, three different Lotus's, each built as a wet-submersible, and each capable of different things to give the range of spectacular effects seen in the film.

The original idea was to use a swish cruise boat for Krest's operation, but that posed too many problems for the art department. Peter Lamont had known and worked with Perry for a number of years and knew of the *J.W. Powell* and its capability of launching independent subs. From photographs, it was clear that the vessel was not quite big enough for the film's purposes. Peter drew a sketch on a photograph of what could be done and, in the *J.W. Powell*'s home port of Riviera Beach (near Palm Beach, Florida), construction work began.

The art department built an extra cabin on to the deck of the boat. Peter did not want it to seem too alien to the rest of the ship and the resulting effect was very convincing. The paint actually looked as if it was chipped. There were rusty rivets (made out of wood) around the windows; even the welding beads (constructed from corking compound) looked realistic. The cabin was stormproof, despite being wooden, but since it would not last any length of time, it was all stripped off after filming. (A small aside here – one of the carpenters working on the construction actually became the ship's cook afterwards.)

As the *Wavekrest*, the *J.W. Powell* sees a lot of action in the film. There were many meetings and discussions about everything concerning both the film's crew and the ship's crew. Before the major scene which involves the ship crashing into the dock, there was a huddle to ensure that none of the flying splinters and falling telephone poles would endanger either crew. 'John Glen doesn't take any chances when it comes to safety,' said Joe, the Captain. 'He's very receptive to any suggestions I offer on how to make an action or something on board appear as it would in reality at sea.'

The whole crew of the *J.W. Powell* were involved in the film and they certainly enjoyed it. And, of course, it is easier to make things look realistic with the real crew performing their functions.

Right: *Pam (Carey Lowell) has taken over piloting the* Wavekrest *while the Captain (Roger Cudney) watches helplessly.*
Below: *The results of Pam's steering are evident when the* Wavekrest *inextricably crashes into the docks, 'I have to admit', said Joe, the Captain of the* J. W. Powell, *'I'm not usually asked to crash through docks but I've had a lot of fun.'*

length	48m (155 ft)
power	1700 horsepower
2 caterpillar main engines	
range	6,000 nautical miles
capacity	40,000 gallons of fuel
accommodation	20 bunks

SANCHEZ' TEAM

Sanchez and Truman-Lodge entertain their guests in Sanchez' luxurious house.

Sanchez has a large and powerful network of people under his control who represent different aspects of his business interests. Politicians, TV personalities, businessmen and hoods are all part of his carefully constructed empire. Indeed, the President of Isthmus City himself is on Sanchez' payroll, needing just the occasional reminder that he is only 'President for *life*', to keep him in tow.

Hector Lopez, the puppet president, is played by Pedro Armendariz, the son of the famous Mexican actor of the same name who left his mark on the Bond series as Kerim Bey, the likeable Turkish agent in *From Russia With Love*. His son, in turn, was a third assistant on the shoot – the first instance of three generations of one family working on a Bond film.

JOE BUTCHER

Joe Butcher is a charismatic frontman for the Olimpatec Meditation Institute, a cult which promotes the secrets of 'cone-power'. His nationwide, live televised fund-raisers for his research institute are used by Sanchez as cover for broadcasting the current price of cocaine to his clients.

Wayne Newton, one of Las Vegas' most renowned singers, plays Joe Butcher. Wayne has sung in Vegas for 30 weeks every year for the last 20 years but has recently turned his hand to acting. 'Film work is quite a departure from what I do literally every night in Las Vegas,' he explained, 'and it's a different kind of pressure and a different kind of challenge. It's great to go to work and be somebody else instead of myself for a while. So I've been really excited about doing this film.'

He is familiar to television audiences as the sadistic prison commander, Captain Thomas Turner in

Pedro Armendariz plays President Hector Lopez, a puppet of Sanchez' regime.

Top: *Joe Butcher (Wayne Newton) makes a televised appeal for his charity while revealing the current prices of cocaine.*
Above: *Pam turns the tables on Butcher after he has lured her to his bedroom.*

ABC's *North and South Book II* – a role he felt at ease with as he was himself born and bred in Virginia. But *Licence to Kill* is special to him. 'We were all raised on the Bond films and it epitomizes what we'd all truly like to believe is out there.'

There is a little bit of Wayne in Butcher, the charismatic charmer who can hold a crowd in the palm of his hand. 'I understand him and his ability to communicate with people. It's one thing to do it on a one-to-one level, it's quite another to communicate to a mass. It necessitates opening oneself up and saying, "Here I am, I'm vulnerable, I do make mistakes but my intentions are honourable." And I feel that way when I'm on stage.' Wayne has tried to find the likeable side of Butcher, believing him to be one of those people who uses whatever means are necessary to achieve a more worthy end.

Wayne is clearly most at home on the stage in front of a live audience. Among his other accomplishments, he is the host of ABC's Cerebral Palsy National Telethon which is, perhaps, where he got his training for his inspired, improvised,

fund-raising speech in the film which was shot at the ceremonial site near Toluca. Even the crew felt some of the force of his stage presence, spontaneously applauding when he had finished.

He has the kind of wealth that makes him a guest on America's voyeuristic TV show, *Lifestyles of the Rich and Famous*. He arrived in Mexico City for the filming in his own private plane accompanied by his fiancee, personal pilot, and hairdresser – a large retinue for someone with a small, albeit important, part. But Wayne is aware that while

he is a big name in Las Vegas, he is hardly known in Europe. He looks to his association with this latest of the Bond films to begin to change all that.

'I was asked to do the Royal Command Performance in England this year but I have never been able to take enough time away from Vegas to go to Europe and do it properly. I think the Bond film will be a great help in opening up that market for me. Anytime people start to recognize you in the street, it's certainly a step in the right direction,' he explained.

TRUMAN-LODGE

William Truman-Lodge, played by Anthony Starke, is the financial whiz-kid of the team. He is a Harvard Business School graduate who is wanted in the United States for insider trading. Before beginning the filming, Anthony carefully researched the part, visiting the financial community, brokerage firms, the Stock Exchange and Harvard. 'It was very interesting, very enlightening,' he told me. 'I had not realized the intensely emotional nature of that kind of work. Many of these guys are very young and there is a high level of burn out simply because it's so emotionally up and down. It is a very gut-level kind of science – not cool and analytic at all.'

Anthony sees Truman-Lodge as somebody who is obsessed by accumulating wealth and making the perfect deal, somebody who is completely suited working for a smart villain like Sanchez. It is Truman-Lodge who gives the long and detailed market analysis of the drug trade to Sanchez' potential clients. The speech, which is full of detailed technical and financial data, is a difficult one to remember but Anthony rarely faltered through several takes. The next day, when they were shooting the scene again, from Bond's point-of-view (outside the window of Sanchez' office), Robert Davi arrived dressed in a subtly different costume, making Anthony (who was always very tense on the set) worried that the scene would have to be reshot. It was the kind of classic wind-up that often takes place on the Bond set.

Chicago-born Anthony is, at 25, only just out of acting school. His first film, a Movie of the Week starring Judd Hirsch, in which he played a quadraplegic, was shot when he was still at college in Milwaukee. He landed a part in the Tom Hanks' vehicle *Nothing in Common* (1986), as a quick-fire assistant in an advertising office and moved to Los Angeles where he has lived ever since.

Anthony said about his part: 'It's sort of a male fantasy to be in a Bond film and I think it's especially fun to be one of the bad guys.'

SANCHEZ' HENCHMEN

Sanchez also has four henchmen, heavies who are at his beck and call to carry out the seamier side of his business transactions. The group have been carefully cast, contrasting different kinds of characters.

DARIO

Benicio del Toro is, at 21, the youngest of the group. He plays Dario, the most vicious of Sanchez' heavies and a dab hand with a knife. Benicio is from Puerto Rico but he moved to Pennsylvania when he was still at school. As a result he is bilingual. He has the kind of smouldering good looks reminiscent of Matt Dillon and he is surely destined to be a hit with the younger Bond fans.

He originally wanted to be a painter. But when he went to the University of California in San Diego he found himself in acting class by mistake – he thought it would be an easy option. He discovered he liked it and was good at it and won a scholarship to Stella Adler's. A part in *Miami Vice* followed and then he landed his first film role: a small part as the dog-faced boy in *Big Top Pee-Wee*. 'But really the Bond is my first movie,' he said, 'because I was a dog in the other one.'

Despite having long hair at the Bond audition, Benecio overcame

Left: *When auditioning for the part of Truman-Lodge, Anthony Starke played a scene from a thriller about a group of ruthless yuppies who killed anybody who got in their way. It was good practice for the part of Sanchez' financial advisor.*

Right: *With his casual good looks, Benicio del Toro who plays Dario has a good chance of stealing the hearts of many of the younger Bond fans.*

Below: *Sanchez' men in action. Dario has got Bond under control while Sanchez is demonstrating his revolutionary techniques for transporting cocaine to look like innocent gasoline.*

the casting directors' worries that he was a bit young and won the part of Dario. 'I see Dario as a dreamer. He's going too fast, taking life for granted. He goes fast in his head, but his movements are slow and calculated except when he's really cornered. He's like an alligator – but he's a young alligator and that's his problem.'

He enjoys Dario's prowess with his knife and went to special classes to get the action right. 'It should be one quick motion. I would like them to show it properly at least once in the film. I think the audience will remember the knife. You want to be the one henchman that everyone in years to come talks about, remembered like Oddjob or Jaws.'

BRAUN

Braun is played by Guy de Saint Cyr, a rugged Mexican born in Cuba. He studied acting for a while, then decided to concentrate on medicine

and acupuncture, becoming involved in a plan to create a comprehensive medical service for the farmers of northern Mexico. But he later returned to drama school, engaging with different methods and styles of acting. He takes his profession very seriously. 'Acting is a thing you study your whole life, he told me. He has done television work including a role in a Mexican soap opera, starring Rebecca Jones, a popular Latin American actress. *Licence to Kill* is his first international film.

Braun looks and acts like a vicious hood. 'He is the kind of person who has buried his natural emotions – he can laugh when someone is dying,' Guy elaborated. 'The responsibility of my performance is to show that he has cut his feelings about everything so he gets into a peculiar way of seeing life. He lives on an island of drugs and perversion. But when I play him, I am proud of being Braun, I don't feel ashamed or bad, I believe that I'm killing for a very

intelligent reason and that we are going to change the world in a very proper manner.'

He is the kind of actor who tries to live the part. In Mexicali, he explained to me, on the third take of a scene in the car chase, he actually felt the petrol on the road beneath the car and knew he was getting angry. He began hitting the steering wheel. It is moments like these when he feels it all comes alive.

So what does his part in the Bond film mean to him: 'It gives me the opportunity to develop the dreams in my life which are to combine my acting with a message to people – anything that helps the world to change in a positive way.' With his medical background, Guy is passionately opposed to all forms of narcotics and heartily applauds the theme of *Licence to Kill*.

Braun usually carries out his orders together with another member of Sanchez' team Perez.

Left: *Benicio del Toro plays Dario, seen here with 007, the youngest henchman to date – and also one of the most charismatic.*
Right: *He proves his metal early on in the film when Sanchez orders him to cut out the heart of Alvarez (Gerardo Moreno) in revenge for his seduction of Lupe, Sanchez' girl. Alvarez is being held by Braun, another of Sanchez' team of trained thugs.*

Below: *Perez (Alejandro Bracho) and Braun (Guy de Saint Cyr) are getting ready to provide a tasty meal for the sharks in the shape of Felix Leiter (David Hedison).*

47

PEREZ

Alejandro Bracho who plays Perez is another Mexican actor. With his lean, hungry looks he makes a striking contrast to Braun. Alejandro comes from a theatrical family – Diana Bracho is a well-known Mexican film actress; an aunt made hats for Marlene Dietrich while Ramon Navarro and Dolores del Rio are both cousins.

He started his acting life in experimental theatre before studying more conventional techniques. But he learned most by doing it – working on the stage for ten years earning no money. He supported himself by translating theatre books and editing a performing arts magazine. He practises Zen and wanted to be a monk before being told that it was incompatible with acting. He sees no contradiction, however, and lives in a temple in Mexico City.

Alejandro prides himself on never playing the same character twice but nevertheless always finding something of himself in the parts he has played. 'It can be scary to find you could be a murderer or something,' he pointed out. Perez is, however, his most vicious portrayal to date.

Perez, he argued, is a contradictory character in that he does not look very threatening – but evidently is. 'He is like a scorpion,' he suggested. 'He does not strike right away, but he waits for a moment with a smirk on his face – he smiles before he pounces.' He hopes this will make Perez more blood-curdling because you never know exactly what he is going to do.

Alejandro, who has just finished filming *Romero* (1989), in which he played a Jesuit priest, is planning to go back to the monastery at the end of filming to recharge his spiritual batteries.

Right: *Heller (Don Stroud) and Sanchez had Bond injured after a fight. It is the proof they need to reassure them that he is on their side. Bond's plan to infiltrate Sanchez' organization has clearly succeeded.*
Below: *Perez, played by Alejandro Bracho, may look mild but he is one of Sanchez' most sinister operatives.*

HELLER

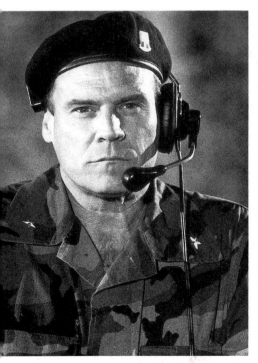

Above: *Don Stroud plays Heller, the head of Sanchez' team of heavies.*

Don Stroud, who plays Heller, the head of security for Sanchez, is from Hawaii and likes to boast that he is the only actor who actually comes from that island. He was a champion surfer – ranking fourth in the world – and it was this ability that first introduced him to films. Troy Donahue was filming the TV series *Hawaiian Eye* and couldn't surf. 'I was about his height and had the same colour hair and when the director asked me if I could surf, I started doubling for him and haven't stopped working since', said Don. He has made around 50 films and over 200 television shows.

Don has never studied acting. He was contracted with Universal and went from show to show. 'That was my training,' he commented, drily. 'This film is going to make something different happen in my life because many people wouldn't see the low budget films that I've done – *The Amityville Horror* (1979), *The Buddy Holly Story* (1978), *The Choir Boys* (1978) and many of the Roger Corman inspired AIP movies.' He has guested in numerous TV series, most recently the Mike Hammer series in which he co-starred with Stacey Keach.

He is tired of being a heavy. 'I usually have to kidnap a girl to get a kiss but I've just had my first romantic lead in a love story *Two to Tango*,' he told me proudly.

Don is extremely aware of the impact even a small part in a Bond can have on an actor's career and has done whatever he can to add to his role. 'It is not a big part but it's turning into something real nice. I either stand beside Tim or Robert so I always get in the shot.' As he speaks Japanese, he asked if he could say some words when Sanchez meets the Orientals. 'I'm dancing as fast as I can,' he joked.

THE BOND GIRLS

PAM BOUVIER

Pam Bouvier is the most modern of the Bond girls so far. Tough and independent, a capable operator in her own right, she is a strong match for 007. Pam is one of Felix Leiter's main contacts in his assignment to nail Sanchez. An ex-army pilot, she has CIA links, having worked with them in Central America.

She is the kind of woman who calls herself Ms not Miss. Her look is very natural, very low key, not like something out of *Dynasty*. With her own assignment and her own plan, she is not at all the traditional female assistant. When, for reasons of cover, she is forced to become Bond's executive secretary, he underlines the difference by ordering her to 'get your hair done and buy some stylish clothes'.

Pam Bouvier (Carey Lowell) is the kind of Bond girl who is equally at home in a bar-room brawl or a ballroom gown.
Left: *In the fight at the Barrelhead Bar she gives as good as she gets – even with Bond at her side.*
Below: *She is one the run in the submarine launching room of the Wavekrest.*

'It's a nice change from the Bond women of the past,' said Carey Lowell, who plays Pam, 'much more contemporary. I've got a great role because Pam is not Bond's little sex kitten – she's saving his life, helping him out and being very independent and self-sufficient in the process. He has an affair with another woman and she's hurt but that's OK. He's just one more man and she can take it.'

Below: *Pam isn't all action – she does manage a few tender moments with 007.* **Left:** *The glamorous side of Pam is evident in this scene at Sanchez' house. No wonder that Carey Lowell was a top model before turning to acting.*

Above: *A production shot from an early scene in the film in which Pam confers with Leiter in his study on his wedding day. The clapperboy is Simon Mills.*

PROFILE

Name: Carey Lowell

Alias: Pam Bouvier
Job description: occasional operative
Bond history: *Licence to Kill*

Carey Lowell is a tall, willowy beauty who has the enviable ability to turn her sensuality on and off at will. In front of the camera, she is as seductive as any Bond girl, but behind the scenes she is modest and unassuming, welcoming the opportunity to merge into the crowd. Between takes she chats amiably or disappears into her trailer to work on numerous pieces of embroidery – a hobby that keeps her calm and unruffled.

She was born in New York but brought up all over the world because her father, a distinguished geologist in the oil business, travelled extensively. As a top model, she lived briefly in Paris but subsequently attended the University of Colorado and later New York University where she majored in literature. She has only 20 credits to go to get her degree

– an ambition that she is determined to achieve.

With clients like Calvin Klein and Ralph Lauren, Carey was at the top of the modelling profession, regularly making the covers of magazines like *Vogue, Glamour, Mademoiselle* and *Gentlemen's Quarterly*, when she decided to go into acting. She took private acting classes through New York's Neighbourhood Playhouse theatre and landed her first film role in 1986: *Club Paradise* starring Peter O'Toole and Robin Williams. 'I was called up with all those beautiful women.' she reminisced. 'They were sitting around with long hair and elegant clothes and furs. I was in jeans and a T-shirt and I thought I'd come to the wrong place.' But at the audition she had to improvize a scene and she won a small part. She spent two months filming in Jamaica. 'I thought, I can do this. I like this lifestyle.'

Licence to Kill is her fifth film. She has acted in two low-budget films for Cannon *Dangerously Close* (1986) and *Downtwisted* (1987). Her most recent venture was a comedy *Me and Him* (1988), starring Griffin Dunne, about a man whose penis starts talking to him. Directed by German film-maker Doris Doerrie, Columbia, who financed the picture, feel it is a bit tricky and they are not sure how to release it in Britain and America. However, in Germany, it has been one of the most successful pictures of 1988.

There may have been a nationwide search for a new Bond girl but Carey was not aware of it. For her it was just like any audition. She did a tape, met associate producer Barbara Broccoli and then John Glen, 'Cubby' Broccoli and the executives from UA. 'It was a simple process,' she recalled. 'I've been to auditions where you have to come back five times. This all happened within two weeks. When I heard I had got the part, I felt, – "Are they sure, are they crazy". I don't see myself in that really sexy image. It's

something I can do, because I know I have the build for it and the looks for it, but it's not how I present myself on a personal level.'

Carey's favourite scene in the film is the one that she initially found most challenging: the confrontation with Bond when he gets her on the bed and holds a gun to her head. 'I was scared of the scene because there's a lot of information to convey that is crucial to the story. Bond's pulling his macho gun stuff blaming me and I know I have all the information to prove him completely wrong and it's great. It is a more equal part which makes it much more interesting. Since Bond has gone out on a limb, he is much less professional than formerly whereas Pam is the professional one. He's on the level of spontaneity or passion, outside the rules, whereas she is playing within the rules.'

Dealing with all the special effects and action in the film, does not seem to throw Carey although she admits to feeling 'more comfortable being glamorous than being tough.' And she obviously had a lot of fun in the scene in the Barrelhead Bar where she becomes a central part of the fight.

So, how does she feel about becoming the new Bond girl She admits to excitement, fear and a little embarrassment, 'because I don't see myself in that sort of way. I like to be anonymous. I can't conceive what's in store for me. I will have to start dressing better – maybe I'll have to wash my hair before even going to the supermarket. I'd like to do something completely different after this, maybe a mother or a hooker. I don't want the image of a glamorous, tough Bond girl to be there forever. I want to experiment.'

But she is also well aware of the tradition that she is stepping into. 'It's like a legacy, I know that I have to live up to the Bond image.'

Left: *The two rivals for Bond's affections, Pam and Lupe (Talisa Soto), meet for the first time in the hotel in Isthmus City.*

Right: *Pam is on the run again, this time from Butcher and his men at the OMI.*

LUPE LAMORA

Sanchez' girl is Lupe Lamora, a former Miss Galaxy beauty, with glamorous, sultry looks. Ambitious for both wealth and powerful men, she came from the kind of poverty-stricken upbringing which leaves her jealous of the diamond collar that Sanchez' pet iguana wears.

Talisa Soto, who plays Lupe, feels that Lupe always knew that she was going to go places. 'She's very at-

tracted to powerful, strong men,' she suggested, but clearly her attitudes are ambiguous. 'Deep down she's a very good person, but she has no way out, involved as she is with this obsessive, crazy man. She does attempt to leave him, but he kills her lover. But she does not realize how evil and vicious he is.' And that, of course, explains why she is attracted to 007 – a strong man who may also provide her with a way out.

Above: *Lupe in the final scene has finally got the iguana's diamond collar. Lupe says to Bond; 'Don't you know iguanas are a girl's best friend.'*

Caroline Bliss plays Miss Moneypenny, M's faithful secretary, for the second time. She replaced Lois Maxwell who had played the part since the beginning. she started on *The Living Daylights* and is back for more. Miss Moneypenny has always been a central part of the story – the office-bound secretary who always has James Bond's interest at heart, whatever the intentions of her boss. Over the years, her constant yearning for 007 has been one of the series' continual ploys.

Caroline is the grand-daughter of the famous British composer, Sir Arthur Bliss. Her debut screen role was as England's favourite princess in the television production of 'Charles and Diana – a Royal Love Story'. A member of the National Theatre Company, she is equally at home playing England's favourite secretary. In *Licence to Kill*, her role is a small but important one. When M suspends Bond from the service, it is Miss Moneypenny who ensures that Bond has the back up and support that he needs.

54

PROFILE

Name: Talisa Soto

Alias: Lupe Lamora
Job description: girlfriend of Franz Sanchez
Bond history: *Licence to Kill*

Talisa Soto has very different kind of looks from Carey Lowell. She has a dark, sultry attraction which looks fabulous given the full glamour treatment. Her natural wide-eyed exuberance is always evident, especially as she punctuates her comments with the occasional wicked wink. At 21, *Licence to Kill* is her second film.

She was born in New York of Puerto Rican parents with Spanish blood on her mother's side, a particularly evocative racial mix. She was brought up in Massachusetts which she remembers as 'lovely but boring'. 'I started modelling when I was 15 with the intention of finding a summer job. It turned out to be a full-scale career move. I was quite lucky, I was not one of those who had to struggle. It happened really quickly for me.' Within a few weeks of her first assignment she was flown to Paris with Bruce Webber, one of America's top photographers. From there she went straight to the top. Webber booked her as often as possible and other jobs followed. She travelled a lot but still returned to school. 'Geography' she grinned. 'Well, I'd been there.' *Harper's Bazaar* magazine rated her as one of the top 18 models of 1988.

She still models, but hopes to move into acting. 'But let's be realistic,' she said. 'If there're no funds coming, we'll have to see.' Her first and only previous film was a low-budget Paul Morissey feature, *Spike of Bensonhurst* (1988) in which she was very 'unglamorized', looking like a little boy with very short hair, sneakers and jeans. She falls in love with a boxer. She received great notices for her small part in a David Lynch, 30-minute short *Cowboy meets Frenchman*, playing a French girl. Acting is not so different from modelling, she argued. 'One is constantly having to perform in front of the camera, surrounded by people. But it is much more satisfying, more stimulating.'

She went through a lengthy process of casting to become a Bond girl, preparing readings, meeting Barbara Broccoli, getting called back, meeting 'Cubby', John Glen, Michael, and others, being screen-tested with four others. 'Finally, when I got the OK, "Guess who's the next Bond girl!" I screamed. My dad is a Bond fanatic so I've seen every Bond film since I was a little kid. This time daddy's going to see his little girl up there,' she boasted.

One of her most difficult scenes was shot on her first day – where Sanchez whips her for being unfaithful. 'I made the nerves work for me, because I was very, very nervous.' But she is also excited about the glamour and the dresses. 'My favourite one is the most stunning, red lace Oscar de la Renta gown which I wear in the casino.' Jodie Tillen, the costume designer, found it but adapted it for Talisa.

'I'm not really crazy about interviews,' Talisa finished with a smile. 'But I love travelling around. I'm really trying hard not to think too much about the publicity and the future.'

Above: *Lupe's power derives from her ability to be seductive. She is the kind of woman who cherishes this power over men.*
Right: *When Sanchez' retreat is under attack from Drug Enforcement Agents (DEA), she has to join the quick escape.*

THE VICTIMS

SHARKEY

Sharkey is a friend of Leiter who has no hesitation in helping Bond to get on Sanchez' trail. A tough, black fisherman who knows the waters around Isthmus City well, Sharkey is a good ally until he is captured and killed.

Frank McRae, a native of Memphis, Tennessee, played American football for the Chicago Bears and the L.A. Raiders before turning to acting. His powerful physique led him naturally to character parts. He trained at the Lee Strasberg Institute, learning the Method School of acting. 'You have to inhabit the character, throw up past emotions and use them to the best of your ability,' he explained. His debut film was John Milius' *Dillinger* (1973), starring former classmate, Richard Dreyfuss, and from there he went on to play a variety of roles including several light comedy parts in films like *Cannery Row* (1982), *Batteries Not Included* (1987) and *Used Cars* (1980), although his ambition is to play a cowboy. He came to Mexico City direct from Malaysia where he had been filming *Farewell to the King* (1988), starring Nigel Havers and Nick Nolte.

Frank was clearly enjoying his time on the Bond film. 'I have a special place in my heart for Sharkey – he's come from a long line of Bond characters that have close ties to Bond through Felix and it costs him dearly because he wants to see justice for what happens to his friend.' He is also aware of it as an extremely good career move – 'This is one picture that I know everyone will want to see.'

Above: *Felix Leiter is, of course, the main victim of* Licence to Kill.
Left: *Poor old Sharkey (Frank McRae) meets a fishy end when he helps 007 to find Sanchez.*

When Sharkey is captured by Sanchez, he is suspended upside-down between two sharks at the back of a boat. Frank McRae, who shot this scene over two days, could not lose the sensation of rocking when he reached dry land. Neither could he lose the inevitable joke, 'Is that all you have to do on this movie – just hang around'

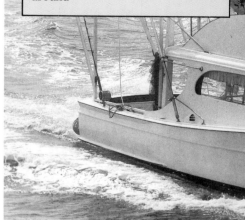

KILLIFER

Killifer, a tough. experienced DEA agent is another of *Licence to Kill*'s victims. Initially, as a colleague of Leiter, he helps with the capture of Sanchez. But the temptations of wealth prove too much for him and he aids Sanchez in his escape from captivity.

Everett McGill, a young, rugged suave-looking actor from Kansas, plays Killifer. *Brubaker* (1980), in which he played one of the prison enforcers was his first film, followed by *Quest for Fire* (1981), the unusual story about pre-historic man told entirely in grunts, and *Iguana* (1988), about an 18th-century man who suffers a terrible facial deformity. Barbara Broccoli had seen Everett's work and brought him to the Bond movie, knowing he would have little trouble with the more physical side of the film.

Frank McRae had worked with Anthony Zerbe some 16 years earlier. He had also previously done a film, *Shaft in Africa*, shot 17 years ago, with Miguel Gil, the first assistant.

Below: *Bond hires Sharkey and his boat to search for the Wavekrest.*
Right: *Killifer (Everett McGill), the treacherous DEA agent, realises he has outlived his usefulness to Sanchez and is about to meet a biting end.*

It could be argued that Killifer is not a usual Bond victim as he works for Sanchez. However, he is a victim of his own greed and earns his place.

THE LOOK OF THE FILM

Traditionally, the Bond films have a lush cinematic feel, with snappy dialogue, pacy editing and fast action. They are also deliberately visually stimulating. Sets, costumes, lighting and make-up are all carefully thought out to add their own important touches to the overall style.

The glamour of the Bonds is tempered nowadays by a real and gritty flavour. There is a more modern, more down-to-earth feel about the latest films, perhaps because Timothy Dalton is a very different kind of Bond from his predecessors or perhaps simply because times have changed. Although the fantastic sound stage creations of Ken Adam, which graced the Bonds of the 1970s with their extravagant sets have gone, the real sets of Acapulco, which Peter Lamont added to, keep up the tradition for glamorous locations and sets. However, some of Peter Lamont's sets are much more bound by the constraints of reality.

Within this general trend, each film has its own special flavour. 'I try to create each film individually,' explained Peter Lamont, the award-winning production designer. 'It is easy to fall into the trap that every-thing is similar.' *Licence to Kill*, set in the drug culture of Central America, has at times an almost seedy quality, particularly evident in the fight scene at the Barrelhead Bar. But the overall effect has a more contemporary flavour.

'Timothy has given us new life,' Peter propounded. In *Licence to Kill*, the *Wavekrest*, for instance, is a real oceanographic ship equipped with a luxury suite. 'Years ago,' Peter explained, 'we would have gone into designing a luxury yacht but now Krest has a certain cover which dictates what the ship must look like.'

58

Opposite: *Krest's laboratory with its aquaria of exotic fish, and tanks of maggots for feeding, is one of the most elaborate of the sets built at the Churubusco Studios.*

Above: *Production designer Peter Lamont is standing in front of the set of Sanchez' office. The exterior is an exact replica of the upper storeys of El Teatro de la Ciudad in Mexico City.*

Below: *The most luxurious location on this film is the private house in Acapulco which was used for Sanchez' house.*

CREATING THE LOOK

Stage one of planning the look of the film is the creation of the storyboard. Director John Glen talks through his ideas with the other key creative personnel and then an artist draws sketches showing how each shot might look. This is particularly important for the action sequences where two, three or even four different units are shooting separate parts of the story, all of which must dovetail neatly together. Then come the location visits and the storyboard begins to take on a shape and a reality.

Peter Lamont has a little book where he sketches his initial ideas for sets and then other members of his department draw them up properly. Models of the sets are made by the art department and then go to the director for approval. He can also use the models to work out his shooting angles and approach to each scene. Finally, blueprints of the designs are drawn up and the art department pass on their concepts to the construction team.

The extent of the work undertaken by the art department is enormous. *The Living Daylights* had between 200 and 240 individual set drawings and *Licence to Kill* even more with around 350. Every little thing seen in the film is designed; even the roads used for the car chases are not all that they seem –graffiti has to be painted out on the surrounding rocks or, on some occasions, new fibreglass ones have to be provided.

At a meeting before the very first film was made, every aspect of James Bond's image was discussed: the kind of clothes he wears, what type of drinks he sips, even down to what kind of lighter he uses. Indeed every part of the film is painstakingly researched in similar detail. For instance, cheques, book jackets and posters all have to be designed especially for the films by the graphic artist in the art department.

59

Ron Quelch, the production buyer, was responsible for commissioning the first gun-metal lighter for Bond on *Dr No*. He had tried everywhere but had no success. In the end, he phoned Dunhill. The sales manager could not believe what was said, for on his desk in front of him was exactly what Ron wanted: – a gun-metal cigarette case and lighter, designed as a Christmas present for a wealthy man. Dunhill have been supplying lighters for the Bond films ever since.

THE SETS

The heart of Peter Lamont's work is with the sets. He is very aware of how much can be done in any particular space. Unlike Ken Adam, whose typically lavish constructions were literally larger than life, Peter works within the dimensions of the building that is being used. 'The real building dictates what happens to the set.'

In *Licence to Kill*, Krest's warehouse is the kind of set – with a shark pool, exotic fish and a tank of maggots – that in the early Bonds might have been a flight of fantasy. Here it is determined by the proportions of the actual building where the exteriors were shot and the result looks very realistic: a working warehouse that makes the villain and his vile intentions all the more menacing.

Or take the mixing room at the OMI where cocaine is diluted with petrol for easy shipment. It is a key set, supposed to be an underground structure with an elevated laboratory where Bond finds himself strapped to a conveyor belt taking him towards a pulverizer in a classically threatening scene at the villain's headquarters. Here Peter was restricted by the size of the Mexican stages which are only 12.5 metres (41ft) high. He had to fit all this into one set and it had all got to work. It is likely to be the largest film set ever built at Churubusco studios.

'I can only build within the space available, so it is a challenge. I have to compromise all the way but I haven't compromised the finish and the quality of the actual sets,' said Peter, proud of his achievements within the limitations that he had set himself.

Above left: *The exterior of Sanchez' office is an exact replica built in the studio of El Teatro de la Ciudad in Mexico City. Even the decorative work has been copied in detail.*

Left: *The art department model of the hull of the* Wavekrest *is a useful tool for the director to plan his shots.*

PROFILE

Name: Peter Lamont

Bond history: *Goldfinger* (draughtsman), *Thunderball* (chief draughtsman), *You Only Live Twice, On Her Majesty's Secret Service* (set decorator), *Diamonds Are Forever* (set decorator), *Live and Let Die* (co-art director), *The Man With the Golden Gun* (art director), *The Spy Who Loved Me* (art director), *Moonraker* (supervising art director), *For Your Eyes Only* (production designer), *Octopussy* (production designer), *A View to a Kill* (production supervisor), *The Living Daylights* (production designer), *Licence to Kill* (production designer).

After leaving art school in 1946, Peter Lamont got a job at Pinewood where he spent two years as a print boy runner earning, as he put it, 'the princely sum of 25 shillings a week.' Then came conscription and he spent two years in the RAF. On his return to civvies, Pinewood was under an obligation to take him back and he became a junior draughtsman. He has literally been working his way up from the bottom ever since. Now, with three Oscar nominations under his belt, he is one of the most renowned production designers in Britain.

Peter Murton, then an art director, introduced Peter Lamont to Bond by asking if he wanted to work as a draughtsman on *Goldfinger*. He only knew of Bond from the *Daily Express* strip cartoons but nevertheless took the job. His first task was to make drawings of the famous set of the inside of Fort Knox for the then production designer, Ken Adam. Peter Lamont has been closely involved with the Bonds ever since. Both Peter Murton and, later in his turn, Peter Lamont became the production designers of successive Bond films. Lamont moved up to set decorator and then to art director and finally he landed the top job on *For Your Eyes Only*. Ken Adam had gone to the States to do *Pennies From Heaven* (1981) and Peter was asked whom he would like to work with as production designer. He replied, 'Why not me?' and there he has stayed.

Peter has always worked on other films in the intervening years between each Bond – *The Ipcress File* (1965), *Funeral In Berlin* (1967), *Fiddler on the Roof* (1971), for which he got an Academy Award nomination, *Boys from Brazil* (1978) and *Aliens* (1986), another Oscar nomination. His third was as part of the team on *The Spy Who Loved Me*.

He has a fund of stories about the various Bonds he has worked on. Like the time he had to learn to swim underwater when he was in charge of the Vulcan bomber on *Thunderball* or the time on *A View to a Kill* when he was literally rebuilding the 007 stage (it had been destroyed in a fire during the shooting of *Legend*, 1985) while they were creating the set for the film's climax – the interior of the mine. His favourite Bond set is probably the underwater one from *For Your Eyes Only* because, as he put it, 'It is such a ridiculous idea.'

Peter enjoys building and designing sets in composite – rooms which always have corridors or other rooms beyond the doors – and revels in the detail. He has worked on some very large sets, including the volcano for *You Only Live Twice*, built on the back lot of Pinewood and reputed to be the largest set ever built. In Mexico, Churubusco's stages are smaller and some compromises have had to be made but he was determined that the quality will not suffer. 'We came to Mexico determined to make Bond as good no matter how difficult because we have a reputation to maintain which we are proud of.'

Above: *Carey Lowell is wearing Pam's practical purple dress – the shortened version.*

Below left: *Playing a modern Bond, Timothy Dalton is not afraid of looking grimy, tattered and torn when the action calls for it.*

COSTUME

According to Jodie Tillen, the costume designer of *Licence to Kill*, 'The Bond films have a certain classic elegance which is an inherent feature of the series.' Her problem was how to translate that elegance to fit the circumstances of this particular story. 'Bond is caught off guard so he's not really prepared for this sort of an adventure. He was going to a wedding and had just a couple of outfits in a suitcase, so we were restricted by reality.' Echoing the thinking behind the sets, the costumes are also designed within the constraints of reality.

'In addition, Timothy has a very clear vision of whom he believes the character to be. So I tried to get into his head and figure out what clothes I could give him that were his alone. He's a very rough and tumble kind of guy, he likes things to be real, to reflect what has happened to him. If he has been running, he wants to be sweaty and rumpled. Sometimes in movies actors just want to be pretty but Timothy has a true feel for making things real. So we make sure we have five or six sets of clothes that are progressively dirtier or sweatier for the appropriate shots. Timothy really wants it gritty.'

Naomi Dunne, Timothy's make-up artist whom he brought with him to the Bonds after working together previously on *The Doctor and the Devils* (1985), agrees with Jodie's assessment of Timothy's way of playing Bond. Timothy, she said, researched Bond in Fleming's books and found out things like the fact that he had long eyebrows. 'He wants to maintain Fleming's image, even in the small details, but at the same time to look real, a Bond who does sweat, does grow stubble and does get his hair ruffled. My task is to give him a warmer colour, accentuating his features and then maintaining that look in all kinds of weather.'

Jodie had a different kind of problem with Robert Davi who plays Sanchez. 'Robert in real life is a man's man and I wanted to put him in an orchid shirt with grey trousers. This caused some trepidation initially but he is so male that it looks beautiful. He made it work for him although he was a little nervous at first. But then he realized it was just a colour, it doesn't change who he actually is.'

Below: *Chief hairdresser Tricia Cameron puts the finishing touches to Diana Lee-Hsu (playing Loti).*

Left: *Robert Davi wearing the orchid-coloured shirt that Jodie Tillen, the costume designer, chose for Sanchez.*

Below left: *Just before shooting the scene in the casino, Carey checks her make-up. The final adjustments are made between each take.*

Below: *Make-up supervisor George Frost, a well-respected technician, checks Robert Davi's appearance before the take.*

THE BOND GLAMOUR

'The women are glamorous and beautiful and elegant and classy,' said Jodie. 'But in this film, the two girls are very different. Pam is all-American – she can do anything, she's willing to take chances, whereas Lupe is a woman who has always had a man to take care of her. She has a pampered life and is always perfectly dressed in beautiful, expensive, rich, sensual, luscious clothes. Even when Pam becomes glamorous, there is a function to the glamour that still has a lean and close style.'

Jodie used the purple, beaded gown that Pam wears to the casino as an example. 'It is a long gown but she can't run fast enough in it so she rips off the bottom of the skirt to make it short. John Glen came up with the idea and it's quite wonderful.' Jodie and her department found out how to make the idea work by trial and error. At first they used velcro but it caught and made lumps. They needed a very smooth join so that the audience is not tipped off that something is going to happen. Then they tried fasteners (160 of them, in total) but they created a ridge and, since the dress is made of faceted beads, the ridge picked up the light. So they created more ridges, making them part of the design of the dress. 'It was very exciting when it finally worked. That for me is the most challenging thing –when the director needs something to behave in a certain way and you try to retain the style and keep the integrity of the outfit while it fulfills its function.'

For Tricia Cameron, the chief hairdresser, working on her first Bond film, *Licence to Kill* has more of an emphasis on being real than she had expected. 'It is not so plastically glamorous as before which actually makes the girls sexier. It is now more natural and less like *Dynasty* than it was.'

By contrast, George Frost, the co-make-up supervisor with Naomi Dunne, is on his fifth Bond. His 40 years in the industry have given him a wealth of experience from *The African Queen* (1951) to *Licence to*

PROFILE

Name: Jodie Tillen

Bond history: *Licence to Kill* (costume designer)

For Jodie Tillen, the costume designer, this is 'the most thrilling job I've ever done in my life'. She stepped into *Licence to Kill* at the last minute when another designer could not make it and could hardly believe her luck. Although she has been the costume designer on films like *Looking for Mr Goodbar* (1977), *No-Mans Land* (1984) and *Night Shift* (1982), (in the latter she had to show a graduation

from hookers to call girls), she acknowledges that this is 'the biggest canvas I've ever had to work on.' Her other claim to fame is that she is one of the originators of *Miami Vice*, the hard-hitting TV cop series.

'I feel that I'm working on history,' she confessed. 'The Bond people have very specific ideas – they've been doing it for years – and on occasion they have had to pull the reins in because I was stepping out of line with what Bond is. And what Bond is, is the most important thing. It took a while for me to get my creativity to work within their vision.

'The whole thing is a logistical nightmare for wardrobe. We have at least 22 different kinds of uniforms and each uniform has maybe 15 pieces. My crew is constantly scrambling to get together all these things.'

Kill. George is one of those people who has worked with everyone there is and as Naomi Dunne said, 'He's a great master of the art, a fantastic man with a fantastic manner.'

George recognizes the important contribution that hair and make-up makes to an artist's confidence, citing John Wayne as someone who would only ever work with his own make-up crew around him. He sees his task on the Bond's as creating a balance between glamour and reality, particularly with the girls. 'They need to look nice but not over-the-top,' he commented.

Jodie Tillen had a lot of trouble designing this dress for Pam. It had to be both glamorous and practical when she gets involved in the action. The result was a multi-layered dress – long for elegant occasions, but shortened when necessary.

64

PROFILE

Name: Alec Mills

Bond history: *On Her Majesty's Secret Service* (camera operator), *The Spy Who Loved Me* (camera operator), *Moonraker* (camera operator), *For Your Eyes Only* (camera operator), *Octopussy* (camera operator), *The Living Daylights* (director of photography), *Licence to Kill* (director of photography).

Alec Mills, the director of photography, has spent his life in the film industry since he left school at 14, apart from serving in the navy for two years. He started as a clapper loader in 1946 at Carlton Hill Studios, then, after his naval service, he went freelance at Pinewood working his way up through the camera grades. He became an operator on *The Saint*, the TV series which of course starred Roger Moore, and stayed as an operator for 16 years. It was the Bonds which gave him the chance to become a director of photography on *The Living Daylights*. Since then he has done several TV commercials and the TV series, *The Dirty Dozen*, where he was the only English person on the camera crew when the film was shot in Yugoslavia.

Although he has worked both as an operator and as a director of photography on several large productions, he nevertheless finds the Bonds the most exciting. They are, he reckons, 'an operator's dream – full of everything.' This is Alec's seventh Bond: he did five as an operator, under Alan Hume, and two as the director of photography. He was working on *King Kong* (1976) when Alan Hume 'got out of step' with the Bonds because he was committed to another film and Alec was offered the chance of promotion. 'If you can imagine how excited I was when I was offered the operator's job, you can begin to understand how I felt when I was made DP.'

Alec's work starts some weeks before the film when he reads the script and visits locations with director John Glen. 'It's walk, walk, walk,' he complained happily. 'At the end of the day you're quite exhausted. It's no holiday.' His task on these reccies is to begin to visualize how to create the right atmosphere for each scene.

Once shooting begins, he has a reputation for keeping cool and calm but 'inside me there's a ball of fire. Inside I die.' On a unit like this where there are four or five different cameramen on the various units, Alec insists that there is no room for egos. It helps having the right mix of people on his crew. He has worked with Michael Frift, his operator, since he was a clapper loader, while Frank Elliott joined the team in 1976 with *The Prince and the Pauper*. 'From then on we got together quite a bit and it worked. The chemistry of the group is vital as we have to work together for some length of time in these conditions. Everyone gets frustrated sometimes but if you have the right blend of people, it helps.' Alec's son, Simon, has joined the camera crew of *Licence to Kill* as the clapper loader because, as Alec was keen to emphasize, he had worked with Michael and Frank before.

'There is always something new, in each film, especially on the Bonds; consequently you always have butterflies.' For Alec, the novelty this time is the underwater work, where he may have to match some underwater interiors to the footage shot by the special underwater crew. But that is clearly what he enjoys. 'There are new challenges, new pressures every time.'

Opposite: *A production still of the camera crew lining up the shot in the mixing room where Bond is conveyed towards the pulveriser.*

Inset: *John Glen and Alec Mills swap angles on the next shot.*

CAMERA

The new approach is also reflected in the lighting of the film. 'There is nothing moody or classical about Bond,' the director of photography, Alec Mills contended. 'I liken a Bond film to a *Boy's Own* magazine and try to keep the image clean. Everything has to be crisp and pristine with a clear, sharp look. When a new Bond comes in we can change the image. For instance, there is slightly less humour now in the Bonds than there was with Roger. I think that this is going to be a very good film with a more gritty style.'

In practice, this means that Alec shoots the film very cleanly, not using bounced light, for instance, but creating hard shadows. He avoids diffusion, rarely using soft lenses, fog filters or low contrast lighting. There was a time, he recalled, when lenses were too sharp and cameramen would try to soften the image. But the anamorphic lenses that Alec uses have an inherent diffusion that creates a tendency towards a more romantic style which he tries to counteract.

'Over the years, the directors of the Bonds have given cameramen the freedom to do what they feel is right. And they have all been first class cameramen. I can't speak for the others but I am trying to do something different. Equally, though,' he insisted, 'I'm not saying any words of wisdom, I just do what every other cameraman does.

'I try to light the villain to make him look more like a villain. If you can get him into a low-key situation, you can get cross lights on him, putting him more in shadow and creating a more sinister atmosphere. Without making him look ugly, you aim to use shadows so that he seems a little more menacing.'

'I'm lucky on this film to have two lovely ladies who are very simple to light. They don't have lines or jowls to disguise so I don't have to soften the light to shoot them.'

THE BARRELHEAD BAR

There is a great fight sequence in *Licence to Kill* which takes place at the Barrelhead Bar, a real dive epitomizing the new look Bond. Pam is sitting at a table in this spit-and-sawdust sleazy bar which boasts a stripper among its many attractions. James Bond comes in and joins her and she reveals that she has a double-barrelled shotgun hidden beneath the table.

A fight starts when some heavies try to strongarm Pam and the locals get involved. Once the fight gets going, it is every man (and woman) for themselves. When things are getting too hot for Pam and Bond to handle, she shoots a hole through the bar wall with the shotgun and the

pair escape thankfully to safety.

Although both cast and crew had great fun filming this scene, it was very demanding for the two principal actors. Timothy, for instance, has to swing across the room on a float above the pool table, kick a guy in the face and swing back again. 'I was standing at the edge of the set,' recalled one crew member, 'and I honestly thought at one point that Timothy was actually hurt. He really looked rough with blood pouring down his face.' It was all very tiring and by the end of the scene, everyone was exhausted with the heat of the set.

Carey, dressed in black with long boots, is as mixed up in the fight as any of the men. As Pam, she has to flip a guy over her head, throw

punches and blow that hole in the wall with her shotgun. 'It amazed me,' she remembered, 'how difficult it is to make that stuff look real, how to make it look as if you are hurting someone without really doing so. Paul Weston was great. He kept telling me to go for it. Some of the actors were saying, "Hit me, hit me." By the end of the scene she had earned the name 'Pambo'.

Gathering together the extras posed problems for Callum McDougal, the second assistant, since Mexicans tend not to be hefty-looking people. But they managed to cast nearly everyone locally –only the stripper was imported from Los Angeles.

The fight was carefully staged to look just right. Paul Weston, the stunt co-ordinator, explained that they had three days to rehearse the fight with all the extras before the filming started. 'That's great,' a member of the camera crew chipped in, overhearing. 'We only get five

Left: *Things are not looking up for 007 when he lands on the floor during the fight while the stripper carries on with the show.*

Left: *A scene from the fight in the Barrelhead Bar, a tough action sequence sprinkled with lighter moments.*

Below: *Paul Weston, the stunt supervisor, demonstrates a move for Carey who takes an active part in the rumpus. It is the first time that Carey has had to undertake this kind of acting.*

minutes to rehearse in.' The whole scene then took four days to shoot. They took a master shot first, then concentrated on filming other bits. At the same time, Keith Hamshere, the stills photographer, was taking pictures of the action. How does he get the pictures with so much going on around him? 'I duck frequently,' he replied.

Paul had at least 25 stunt people as customers in the bar and a further 50 extras to work with. He knew the ground Bond had to cover and planned the fight aiming to use as much floor space as possible. He had to consider factors such as putting Bond in the best possible light and the kinds of things that Pam might be capable of doing. He had breakaway chairs and sugar-glass bottles and glasses to help him. He then worked it all out in rehearsal, using all the props plus the possible areas. 'It's important,' he explained, 'to put it all where the camera can see it. Therefore you concentrate the action around the principals.' He found the sequence very enjoyable. 'Everyone had a great time and really got into it. We had to shout out "cut" several times.'

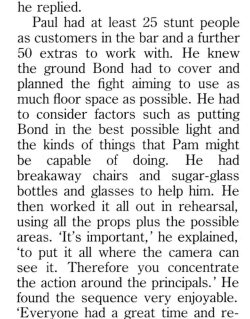

Below: *Bond has never been the kind of man to pull his punches – and he is not likely to start now.*

The special effects boys developed a specially shaped charge to blow the hole in the wall. They placed this on the wall and also had hooks built in so that they could pull everything out at the instant of the blast. Two cameras filmed the action at different speeds to create the right effect. The net result was to make it look as if everything were exploding outwards.

'I was right there when they did it,' said Harris R. Bierman, the armourer who is, after all, used to this sort of thing. 'It was absolutely amazing.'

PUTTING THE PRODUCTION TOGETHER

WHY MEXICO?

Above: *Carey seizes a rare opportunity to see for herself what things look like from the other side of the camera.*

Before work had even started on the new film, it had become clear that it would be too expensive to shoot *Licence to Kill* at Pinewood Studios, near London, the home of the Bonds for so many years. The differential of the pound to the dollar, meant that both the production and the distribution company felt that the cost of making the film in England was too high. Given the Latin American flavour of the story, it made sense to find a new studio base in that part of the world. The Bond team bid a reluctant farewell to Pinewood Studios, only returning for the post-production of the film.

After some preliminary reccies in China proved that it was too logistically complicated a place to film in, Mexico became a possible option. Douglas Noakes, the film's accountant, went out there and made an

extensive financial survey of the facilities. In the end, it was the cost factor that was decisive. He found a lot of stage space, an apparently well-serviced studio and cheaper labour than elsewhere. As Barbara Broccoli summed it up, 'There aren't many places in the world where all that comes together.' Michael G. Wilson, John Glen, Peter Lamont, Barbara and Tom Pevsner flew around Mexico looking for likely locations, satisfied themselves that they could film *Licence to Kill* there and moved the production, lock, stock and barrel to Mexico City.

Right: *John Glen and Michael G. Wilson take advantage of some of the local facilities in Mexico City – the kind they are unlikely to find within reach of Pinewood Studios.*

CHURUBUSCO STUDIOS

Churubusco Studios were built in the 1940s by Howard Hughes and the back lot still has the remnants of his Wild West towns. He sold the studios to private Mexican investors after the war and during the 1970s it was bought by the Mexican government in whose hands it remains. While some Mexican producers have permanent offices there, the studios are being used more and more frequently by foreign production companies who are attracted by the relatively cheaper costs of filming in Mexico. *Licence to Kill* is probably the largest film to have been shot at Churubusco even though films like *Dune* (1984) have also been shot there, but they did not have the complexity of so many different units filming at the same time.

Hector Lopez, the Mexican production supervisor on the film, was aware that for both him and the studio it was a very special opportunity. 'It's a unique kind of film to be working with. *Licence to Kill* pro-

vides an important source of funds for the studio and for the people it is both work and a learning experience. I've worked all over the world for 27 years, but never on a film like this with so many sets, so many people,' Hector commented. He believes, a little tongue-in-cheek perhaps, that the main difference between different units in different countries is the time they take to eat lunch.

Above: *The Kenworth Truck Company tankers for use in the final sequence were all prepared at Churubusco Studios. They then had to undertake a journey of several days to get to the location in the far north of Mexico.*

Below: *The restaurant at the studios. The whole ambience of Churubusco is quite different to that of Pinewood. For instance, every stage has its own shrine in the corner.*

THE SCHEDULE

Having decided to base the film in Mexico City, the next task for the production team was to budget and schedule the film. This was primarily the responsibility of Tom Pevsner and Barbara Broccoli, the associate producers. The Bonds are virtually unique in knowing their release dates before they go into production. United Artists always have an accurate idea of when they want to release the films so the schedule for filming is worked backwards from that date.

It was originally intended to release *Licence to Kill* at the end of May 1989 in the States but the dates changed during filming to the middle of July. However, the UK will see the first showing which will be a Royal charity premiere for The Prince's Trust with the Prince and

Princess of Wales in attendance.

Otherwise the schedule is built around the weather conditions of the various locations and around the specific problems of the art department. 'As a pattern,' Tom explained, 'we know that the Bonds have on average a new set every day and a half throughout the film which puts a tremendous strain on the construction department. The only way they have any chance of keeping up is by scheduling to switch continually between studio and location shooting.' Thus *Licence to Kill* started shooting in the studio in July and had to go to Key West in August which was not the ideal time because of the rains. After that they returned to the studio, then on local location in Mexico City, back to the studio once again, then to Acapulco and finally back to the studio for the last time. Meanwhile, wardrobe and

casting were done in Los Angeles while the 2nd unit went to Key West and Mexicali, the underwater unit to Cancun and the aerial unit to Key West, all of which had to be dovetailed into the master plan. It was no easy task to make it all fit.

In many ways, the Bonds are, what Tom referred to as 'primitive film-making'. There are no great optical effects or technical tricks with the result that the films can be put together as they go along. Laboratory work can be time-consuming and there is no space for that kind of process on the tight schedule of the Bonds. They, in fact, do almost everything for real. 'We try hard to do things in such a way that the actual actors can do them to avoid process work,' Tom confirmed. This is not, of course, purely a logistical decision; part of the charm of the Bonds is due to this essentially sim-

ple approach to film-making, seen here at its best and producing a straightforward adventure without recourse to visual wizardry.

The film is edited and put together while it is being shot. A rough dub is made as they go along with music cut in from previous Bond films, so that the financiers and the publicity people have something to view. This is another complex facet of the tight production schedule of these films and another indication of the vast difficulties that are caused if the production slips a day or two behind schedule.

Below: *This production still shows just how big the 'mixing room' set at the studios was. Pam and Bond are fleeing from an imminent explosion.*

Below right: *The call sheet for the first day's shooting of* Licence to Kill.

PROFILE

Name: Tom Pevsner

Bond history: *For Your Eyes Only* (associate producer), *Octopussy* (associate producer), *A View to a Kill* (associate producer), *The Living Daylights* (associate producer), *Licence to Kill* (associate producer).

Tom Pevsner, the associate producer of the Bond series since *For Your Eyes Only*, is the son of Sir Nikolaus Pevsner, the famous architectural historian who has written the definitive work on British buildings. After serving in the army during the Second World War, Tom graduated in modern languages from Cambridge University.

He began in the film industry in 1951 as a third assistant with Sir Michael Balcon at Ealing Studios, rising to first assistant on Ealing classics like *The Ladykillers* (1955). He has sinced worked with some of the great names of cinema: John Huston, John Ford, Billy Wilder and many others.

He moved from being a first assistant to the production side when he became associate producer on Alexander Mackendrick's *A High Wind in Jamaica* (1965) and Fred Zinnemann's *Julia* (1977). When John Glen became the director of the Bonds, Tom, with his wealth of varied experience, was an obvious choice to head the production side. He brought in many of his own people who have remained with the Bonds over the last five productions.

According to Barbara Broccoli, the other associate producer on the film, Tom 'supplies the brain' behind the production. 'He is a highly educated, creative, talented man who thinks everything out logically and then acts on it, pushing himself and the people around him to get things done.'

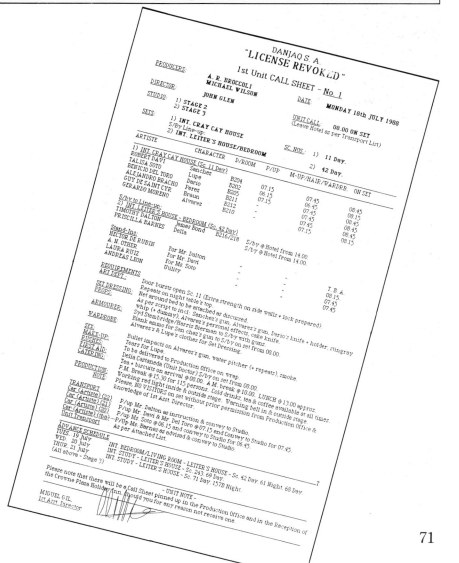

MOVING IN

The new art department was especially built for the crew at Churubusco. It is one of the facilities that has been left behind for future film-makers to use.

Working from Mexico made the production even more difficult than usual. The first four weeks of pre-production were, as Tom put it, 'just housekeeping'. Churubusco turned out to be little more than a hollow shell and the production team had to bring in everything from scratch: telephones, typewriters, fax machines and so on. When they went, they left behind a fully-equipped production office which they hope somebody will buy.

Other problems beset them. Tom reckoned that at one point he counted 177 leaks in the roof. Nevertheless, by the time the shooting crew arrived, the production office was in full working order.

The art department had similar problems. There was nowhere suitable for them to set up drawing boards and models. The existing art department space was cramped and damp, so they built a complete new pre-fabricated department which is light and spacious and will remain as an asset to the studio.

The stages, themselves, presented another type of hurdle. Over the years, the stages had been needed at different heights but they had been built not with wood as they would have been in England, but with concrete. One stage, alone, needed 80 cubic metres (105 cubic yards) of concrete to level it up. And *Licence to Kill* shot on seven of the eight Churubusco stages.

There was a notice on the refrigerator in the production office at Key West: 'your mother is not necessarily working here – clean up after yourself'.

THE PRODUCTION OFFICE

The production office was always a hive of activity with telephones constantly ringing and people going in and out. Here they dealt with every aspect of filming and living in Mexico City, from flying the whole crew and equipment to Key West to the daily arrangements for laundry. When the crew goes on location, the production office goes with it. On one particular July day, for instance, they were supervising building in Mexicali, preparations in Mexico City, shooting in Cancun and two units in Key West, ensuring that, in each case, all the myriad little details were being taken care of. It is literally a 24-hour-a-day job.

Most of the current production team came to the Bonds after *Moonraker* when a new director, John Glen, started and Tom Pevsner came in as the associate producer. The Bonds had been getting more and more expensive and it was a policy decision to return to the formula of the earlier films. *For Your Eyes Only* represented not only a change of style for Bond but also a change of personnel.

Tony Waye, the production supervisor, is one of the people who joined the crew at that time. He was the first assistant director on *For Your Eyes Only*, subsequently promoted to production manager and then production supervisor with the later films. Tony, who started in the industry as a mailboy at Pinewood, spent 21 years as a first assistant, working on over 60 films from the Carry Ons to *Star Wars* (1977). It is the kind of 'hands-on' experience which is invaluable in the production office.

Tony and his team dealt with all the logistics of the shoot. 'I hold together and control all the movement of equipment, transport, crew, props and actors,' he explained. He dealt with all the day-to-day details and was usually to be found submerged in paper; he had lists of everything. He weighed the costs of different ways of doing things, set up many of the deals and generally had the responsibility of keeping things within the budget. 'As Tom Pevsner called me on my application form for a work permit in America, I am the nuts and bolts man,' he joked.

Whether in Pinewood or Mexico, the production department is always beset by problems. Iris Rose, the unit manager, contends that the continuity of crew, particularly of heads of department, makes it easier because they all know how things are done on the Bond films. On the other hand, being based abroad means learning the different laws, regulations, customs and habits of another country.

Mexico City is in the heart of mañana country which meant that the biggest production headache was that even if somebody had promised that something would happen, you could never be quite sure it would until it actually did.

As any delays in filming cost a fortune, everybody was therefore having to allow more time than usual for preparation, in case things did not turn out right the first time. In addition, bureaucracy was rampant making it difficult to obtain the necessary permits from the government offices, the army, the customs officials and others in authority.

Tony Waye put his diary and notes down one day when visiting the location in Key West. His notes contained all the information he had been amassing from various people about the numerous different requirements of the three units then shooting. He was still talking when a helicopter landed on the set and a great gust of wind blew his notes into the water. One of the girls on a nearby boat dived to the rescue and saved production's day.

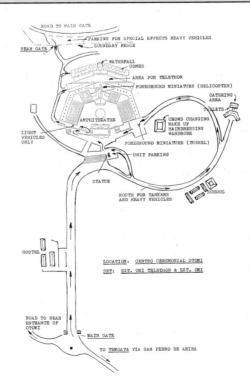

Above left: *The logistics of shooting on every location have to be planned down to the smallest detail. This production map of the Otomi site at Toluca is an example of the precision of the planning.* **Above right:** *Tony Waye, the production manager, is on location, typically equipped with a pile of notes and questions for the crew.*

THE UNIONS

Licence to Kill was shot in Mexico and America with Mexican, American, English, French and Spanish crews – all of whom have different union regulations covering their overtime, their mealbreaks and their per diems. It is an accountant's nightmare. In Mexico, it is joked, the unions, which were formed later than the film unions in other countries, read the rule books from around the world and then extracted all the best parts to include in their own conditions of work. They have, for instance, a national holiday to celebrate the founding of the union.

Left: *It was probably the large cigars that Sanchez smokes that inspired this piece of clowning on the set from Robert Davi. Jokes and gags are a regular feature of the Bond set.*

74

Each studio has its own technicians' union and actors' union. Tony Waye found that, despite their stringent rules, the unions were always ready to negotiate and discuss and compromises could be reached where necessary. The unions had people who understood the exigencies of film-making and while in some respects he found they were very old-fashioned, in others they were reasonable.

Outside the film unions, other union problems were not so simple. When the charter plane from Key West landed at Mexico City airport, the production office had mini-buses standing by to meet the crew and transport all the equipment. But taxis have an exclusive franchise at the airport and the drivers put a chain across the entrance, refusing to allow the minibuses to leave until they had paid a toll. At the end of each day's shooting, the supervisor passes that day's output.

THE GOVERNMENT SUPERVISOR

Every foreign film shot in Mexico has to have a government supervisor from the State Department attached to it (although the actual person seems to change every four weeks). Their job is to oversee the script content to ensure that the film is not showing Mexico or Latin America in a derogatory light. And, at the same time, they keep an eye on the sex and violence elements. The government supervisor has the power to intervene in the shooting at any time but, in practice, the relatively few problems are sorted out with a quiet word to the director or producer.

Their input in the film is not solely to do with censorship. It was a government censor who spotted a Mexican Aeroclub sticker on a supposedly Isthmus City plane as one scene was being shot.

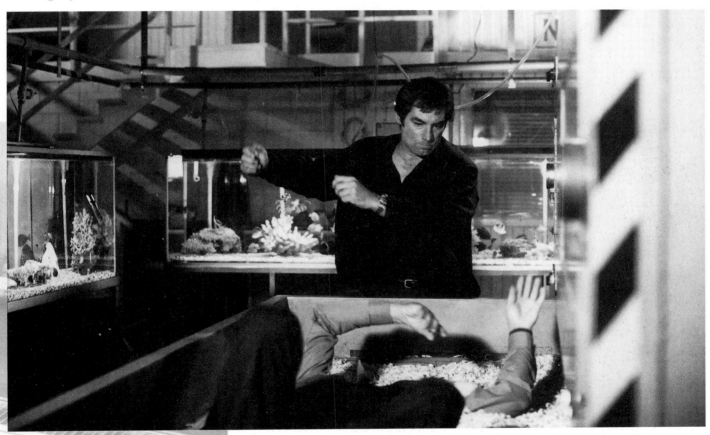

Above: *One of the most elaborate sets built at Churubusco was Krest's marine biology laboratory. Here Bond discovers that this is where Leiter had his encounter with a shark but is surprised during his searches by one of Sanchez' operatives. Bond finds the maggot tank the most appropriate repository for his assailant.*

Left: *The largest set for* Licence to Kill *was the mixing room underneath the OMI centre. It had to be big enough to allow the tankers to drive right into it – and out of again.*

Below: *Director John Glen discusses the action with Carey Lowell for her scene in the launch room of the* Wavekrest.

THE DOCTOR

'Cubby' Broccoli, according to Dr James D'Orta, wanted to treat the crew like a family and insisted on providing what he called 'the Gold Standard' of medical care while they were in Mexico City. Dr Jim, as he was known to the crew, is part of Lifestar International, an organization which specialises in providing medical services to film units. There was a rota of four doctors each of whom was certified as an emergency physician and each of whom practised elsewhere and therefore could not afford to be with the unit full-time.

Dr Jim is an associate clinical instructor of emergency medicine at Georgetown University, Washington. He is also 'Cubby's' cousin. He did his medical training in Mexico and, since he knows the area well, he headed the US relief team to the earthquake a few years ago. Shortly after the completion of shooting, both Dr Jim and his colleague Claude Cadoux, another member of the Bond team, flew to Armenia to assist the emergency crews in operation there after the earthquake. The White House publicly saluted their action. *Licence to Kill* is Dr Jim's second Bond film and he is very much part of the family. Stories abound about him, like the time he removed all the crews' moles in Morocco.

But the medical care of the unit has a more serious side. Before the unit came to Mexico, Lifestar International did a lot of pre-planning. They tested blood supplies and water sources and set up an emergency evacuation programme in the event of a major disaster. The doctors were always on hand on the set and had stores of the newest and most expensive drugs and other supplies to deal with almost all emergencies. They even examined the catering arrangements to ensure the food was both balanced and hygenic. This level of care, of course, not only provided the crew with first class medical facilities but also reduced the insurance premium.

Dr Jim is adamant that the medical team was not only concerned with

Above: *Dr James D'Orta in his medical domain – an important off-screen facility for the welfare of the cast and crew while they worked in Mexico City.*

Below: *Dr Jim also managed to get a taste of what it is like in front of the camera as he plays one of the guests at the casino where Pam and Bond have gone to find Sanchez.*

PROFILE

Name: Barbara Broccoli

Bond history: *Octopussy* (executive assistant), *A View to a Kill* (additional assistant director), *The Living Daylights* (associate producer), *Licence to Kill* (associate producer).

Barbara Broccoli is 28 years old, which made her exactly one year old (to the day) when her father, 'Cubby' Broccoli, signed the first Bond deal for *Dr No* with United Artists. She has literally grown up with James Bond and has an instinctive feel for the films and the crew.

She majored in motion picture and television communications at Loyola University, Los Angeles, and has worked her way through many of the departments of the unit. She started as a third assistant director – a classy title for somebody who runs messages, handles walkie-talkies and directs traffic. She also worked in the publicity and casting departments of Eon Productions. 'I wanted to be like Dad,' she confessed, 'so it's important to know what everybody does – and that you can only find out by doing the job yourself.' She was made an associate producer on *The Living Daylights*.

Barbara is centrally involved in the casting of *Licence to Kill*. 'It is exciting to find new actors on the verge of being discovered.' She is clearly thankful that the Bonds are not hampered by the need for big name stars like many international movies. 'I like to find a casting director who's flexible and does not use the same names all the time but draws from various areas – cinema or theatre.' Her knowledge of actors is considerable but she also deals with the contracts, sorting out the preliminaries before turning over the details to lawyers.

Looking after the actors is by no means her only responsibility. Her other traditional area is the 2nd unit where she is commonly known as the big sister of the crew, endlessly cheerful, solicitous of everyone's problems and fighting for the resources for the unit to do its job. 'I prefer the rough-and-tumble of location shooting to the air-conditioned production offices,' she confessed. And on that shoot, she has the same ability to inspire loyalty that her father has.

Barbara works full-time on the Bonds. As she finishes the promotions on one film, the reccies start on the next. But she would really like to make another film, of her own, between Bonds, perhaps a low-budget feature in England.

---

emergencies. It also developed a 'wellness' programme to keep the crew stable in their many months away from home. In the polluted atmosphere of Mexico City, gastroenteritis and bronchitis are the two most common deseases. Dr Jim also had to deal with ligament injuries, lacerations. dehydration, cardiac problems, and in one case a person suffering from a serious hypo-thyroid condition. The high altitude and polluted atmosphere of Mexico City exacerbates every kind of health problem.

'Timothy calls us "the touch of reality in a world of make-believe",' said Dr Jim one day on the set when he had been coaxed to the front of the cameras to play a patron of the casino. 'This allows me to share their world but they can't share mine.'

PROBLEMS OF FILMING IN MEXICO

Many of the day-to-day problems of filming in Mexico arose from working somewhere that was not used to the demands of a large unit. While no-one had anything but praise for the Mexican film crew, the lack of any sense of urgency outside the studio made life increasingly difficult.

Michael Ford, the set dresser, and Ron Quelch, the props buyer, had some of the most frustrating tales. They often found the simplest things difficult. There are no property hire companies in Mexico so everything had to be found in the shops. Door furniture, for example, became a major headache. The key to Joe Butcher's bedroom plays an important part in the plot and the lock on the door had to be just right. Ron and Michael saw the lock they wanted used as a decoration in a shop, but they could not find it for sale anywhere. Eventually the film's carpenters made them the locks they wanted. 'When you see the film,' said Michael, 'you'll see that all the doors have the same handles. You have to have a sense of humour, don't you?'

Or take another problem: the construction department ordered 1000 washers. They were asked what washers were and explained that they were the bits of metal that fit on to screws. The washers duly arrived – round pieces of metal without any holes in them.

Tom Pevsner and Michael Wilson, towards the end of the shoot, discussed how they thought it had gone, taking an overview of it all. Tom estimated that the shooting, itself, had taken 40 per cent longer than it would have done at Pinewood. Although they finished shooting on schedule it was at the cost of sometimes very long days. On the other hand, the construction of the sets had taken less time than they thought. The crews were excellent; they found some superb craftsmen, who had no problems meeting dates, even coming in early, and the finishes were first class. Overall, it was undoubtedly cheaper to film in Mexico City and Tom felt the decision to move there had been vindicated. He did, however, find this a difficult conclusion to reach as he personally had not enjoyed the experience.

Michael G. Wilson echoed Tom's conclusions. While there is nothing actually to compare the budget to, as this Bond was not made at Pinewood under the new conditions, other comparable films shooting at the same time have cost more. *Batman* (1989), made at Pinewood, was budgeted at $40 million and the new Indiana Jones adventure at over $50 million, whereas *Licence to Kill* is estimated at $35 million.

ON LOCATION

KEY WEST

Right: *Governor Bob Martinez of the state of Florida clearly enjoyed his visit to the set in Key West.*

Key West, the last of the 150-mile stretch of coral islands that extend westwards into the sea off the coast of Florida, was the location for a month's filming. Scenes set in Key West itself, like the wedding sequence, were shot there. With its Spanish-style wooden slatted houses, open verandas and tropical vegetation, it has a Latin American flavour, which also made it suitable for some of the film's Isthmus City scenes.

Filming in Key West was not without its problems – many of them unforeseen. Intermittent power cuts, affecting the whole island, and occasional water failures, added to the difficulties, while it rained so much, that it was referred to as 'Key Wet' on the call-sheet one day.

Florida, which wants to build up its reputation as a centre for the film industry, was keen to have the shoot on its territory. Governor Bob Martinez, a Republican, visited the set and spent an hour or so with the crew. A self-confessed Bond fan, he presented 'Cubby' Broccoli, Michael G. Wilson and worldwide head of marketing, 'Jerry' Juroe each with the Great Seal of the State of Florida. Shooting came to a standstill as the set was besieged with hordes of pressmen, photographers and aides who were 'more complex and useless than anything on a film set,' according to one spectator. The Governor was given his own director's chair, and the traditional photographs were taken as he clapperboarded the next shot.

Later, the governor won a walk-on part in the film. He appears briefly as a customs officer in the scene at Key West airport. The governor and his wife made an official visit to Britain during the post-production of *Licence to Kill* and while in Britain, they visited Pinewood and met the Bond team once again. As a gesture of thanks for the co-operation of the State of Florida, 'Cubby' and Michael arranged for three charity screenings of *Licence to Kill* in the State capital, Tallahasee.

The Honky Conch Cafe or Harbour Lights Bar provided the front for the Barrelhead Bar in the film. A false wall was built for filming and a seedy neon sign hung in place but the owners of the bar want to keep both as a tourist attraction. They are thinking of renaming it the Barrelhead Bar.

Left: Governor Bob Martinez (centre) presents Michael Wilson (left) and 'Cubby' Broccoli with bronze seals for the state of Florida, during some night filming in Key West.

Mallory Square in Key West's old town where, just before sunset every evening, jugglers and snake-charmers entertain the crowds while local artists sell earrings and pictures in the narrow cobbled streets. Hundreds of people gather in the square to watch Florida's romantic sunsets. It was here that Bond is told by DEA agent Hawkins to lay off the Sanchez case.

79

KEY WEST MAP

The cast and crew danced and had a good night out one Saturday in Sloppy Joe's Bar, the bar where Hemingway used to drink in Key West. It is a wild place full of extravagant rumours. The night in question, the band struck up the 007 theme as a greeting.

The Coastguard Pier was where the *Wavekrest* was moored and many of the scenes were filmed including the *Wavekrest* crashing into the dock. It was also the boarding point for the boats to Snipe Point, a mangrove area that is a nature reserve full of wild birds and turtles.

US1 which runs from the US/Canadian border in Maine to Key West, is the longest highway in America. The publicity office was the first (or the last) house on the road.

The production office, situated – not unnaturally – in Fleming Street.

The Hemingway House, 907 Whitehead, is where Hemingway lived for 30 years until his death in 1961. The veranda of this Spanish-style house is where M revokes Bond's licence to kill and asks him to turn in his Walther PPK. It is Bond's 'farewell to arms'.

St Mary's Star of the Sea Catholic Church where the wedding was filmed is the second oldest church in the USA. Father Quinlan of the local church actually played the priest in the film's wedding service.

There are no cellular mobile telephones in Key West as the relay systems do not stretch this far down the keys. This, of course, left the crew with a communications problem, having to rely on walkie-talkies and public phone boxes.

Map labels: ISTHMUS HARBOR · PIER 3 · COASTGUARD HQ · PIER 2 · PIER 1 · KEY WEST BIGHT · US NAVEL STATION · MARINA CIGARETTE BOAT · LA CONCHA HOTEL · FLEMING STREET · SOUTHARD STREET · ANGELA STREET · PETRONIA STREET · OLIVIA STREET · CHURCH · FRANCES STREET · WHITE STREET · PALM · GEOR... · TRUMAN AVENUE · UNITED STREET · SOUTH STREET · WASHING... · LEITERS HOUSE AND PATIO (STEPHANO'S HOUSE) 707 SOUTH ST.

80

Garrison Bight is where the deep sea fishing boats run daily, taking sightseers to the protected waters of the reefs. It is here that Bond meets Leiter's fisherman friend, Sharkey.

Key West and the adjacent islands are popular with fishermen. There are innumerable protected channels and reefs in which to fish for snapper and tarpon while stingrays, barracuda and dolphins are also common. Over 600 varieties of fish are in these waters including the conch, whose shell has given its name to the people and the area.

Turtle Kraals where the sea-turtles are kept, became the place where Bond has the pilot boat is moored. The Half Shell Raw Bar has an ancient ship's bell which is rung in recognition of large tips.

The world's biggest undersea treasure trove was found off the Key West coast in July 1986. Spanish treasure worth $341 million, stolen from the Indians in Carahagna and dating from the 1500s, was recovered. The ship, which had been hit by two hurricanes before foundering on the reefs, had evaded searchers for some 20 years and its discovery was a national event. Many of the divers involved found jobs on the Bond shoot.

THE US COAST GUARD

For three weeks, the Bond crew had full access to the facilities of the US Coast Guard at Key West. The *Wavekrest* was moored at their pier – it later crashed into the dock there. Their helicopters and pilots were used in several sequences. Their base even became the staging post for the shuttles out to the *Wavekrest* when it was anchored some miles off the key itself. In fact, the Coast Guard became generally indispensable to the action sequences filmed at Key West.

Co-ordination between the film and the Coast Guard was the province of Commander John McElwain USCG, a tall all-American type who looked completely at home on the James Bond set. John is the head of the Coast Guard's Hollywood liaison office and his job takes him to film sets around the country. In the last year he has worked on the Faye Dunaway thriller *Midnight Crossing* (1989), shot in Miami, the Goldie Hawn comedy *Overboard* (1988) shot in Los Angeles and New York and a variety of TV programmes like *Falconcrest* and *Miami Vice*. He was attached to the James Bond unit for the duration of its stay in Key West.

Whenever they are asked to participate in a movie or television programme, the Coast Guard realize that it is in their interests to have somebody on location to make sure that they are accurately portrayed. They are highly image-conscious and recognize the role that films can play in bringing them to the public's attention.

'We'd like the people in the Mid West to understand where their taxes go,' explained John. 'The Coast Guard's public relations effort is many-pronged. Unfortunately, unlike many other government agencies, we don't have a lot of dollars to tell our story. We don't have an advertising budget. We do have a very small recruiting budget but it doesn't go very far. We produce public service announcements but we don't have any money left to buy airtime for them – so they are likely to go out at the end of the evening with the National Anthem and therefore have a limited impact.

'We understand the importance of movies. If we can get a few young people to look at our role in this movie, for instance, and see what we're doing, see our technology and think they'd like to be a part of it, then that is in our interests. There's a direct relationship between performance and what a congressman – or his constituents – sees and the dollars that come towards our organization.'

The Coast Guard recognize that they have an image problem. They are involved in so many different areas that most Americans are not really sure what they do. In the movies they may be ice-breaking,

Above: *Bond has just thrown the pilot out of the plane in order to fly it himself.*

Left: *Before any shot involving the helicopters, the whole crew would go off into a huddle to discuss the action and the possible problems. Commander John McElwain is in uniform at the centre of the group and the eagle-eyed may be able to recognise the author of this book at the edge – taking notes as always.*

or be a part of the military defence of the country. They might deal with oil or chemical pollution or other environmental duties, with fisheries' enforcement and the searching of vessels, or with aids to navigation. They are also a rescue agency, dealing with accidents at sea and even the drought problems of the Mississippi river fall within their remit. 'We're everywhere,' said John.

In this movie they are primarily law enforcement officers. 'We're also very competent helicopter pilots and able to handle the latest technology in a way that should be exciting to young people,' John explained.

But the Coast Guard are also very careful to protect their reputation and insist on script approval before they become involved in a film. They shy away from heavy-handed law enforcement parts where, for instance, they go aboard a vessel and shoot it out. They want the agency to be portrayed accurately although they do appreciate that reality sometimes needs to be stretched a little for artistic reasons. 'There are things in this film, for instance, which a pilot knows are impossible but which the magic of the movies makes real.'

At an early stage of *Licence to Kill*, the Coast Guard were asked if they would be the armed personnel in the troop carriers accompanying the armoured truck in the convoy that takes Sanchez to prison. 'They hoped we would be able to do it with our blue uniforms and law enforcement image,' recalled John. 'I said

frankly that that was out of our jurisdiction.' John was, however, able to recommend which outfit would be appropriate.

'Once we sign an agreement to participate in a film we become part of the film company. But we never relinquish total control. Our pilots always fly our planes and they won't do so if they think safety is an issue. But once we are on the shoot, most problems are logistic ones.' John's department looks after the licences, the agreements, the insurance and the other details of filming permissions.

Not all the films John works on are as concerned with authenticity as *Licence to Kill*. There have been times when he has taken his boats and his helicopters and gone home. At other times, he has required actors to get their hair cut so that they actually look like military personnel.

The Bond crew, however, is 'extraordinarily reasonable, co-operative and understanding.'

One final word. However involved in a film the Coast Guard become, it is never allowed to interfere with normal operations. As John put it, 'We are life-savers first, film-makers second.'

> The US Coast Guard is an agency of the Department of Transportation. It is not part of the Department of Defence even though it is an armed military force. Its role is essentially a humanitarian one. There are only 39,000 in the Coast Guard nationally, which is less than the staff of the New York Police Department.

THE PLANES

Aerial sequences are another staple ingredient of the Bond diet. Each aerial stunt is carefully planned, taking into account factors like wind, heat and altitude. In Mexicali, for instance, where the crop-duster sequence was shot, the altitude varies from below sea level to 1262m (4100ft) above it, with significant changes in temperature. This means that shooting preferably has to take place either early in the morning or late afternoon.

Corkey Fornof is a very crucial figure in the tanker sequence that takes place in Mexicali, flying a lightweight plane through a series of dangerous and impressive manoeuvres. 'But its fun when it all pulls together,' he said.

With all the planning in the world things can still go wrong. 'Everyone wants to come and look at the stunt,' Corkey moaned. 'You have to file notice with the aviation authorities in order to film and it's like placing an ad. And then they look at the camera and wave.'

THE SEA-PLANE SEQUENCE

One of the most unusual stunts in *Licence to Kill* involves 007 water-skiing behind a sea-plane. It needs an expert skier to execute a difficult set of manoeuvres; perfect weather conditions when the sea is not too rough for skiing but slightly choppy for the plane to be able to land and take off; and an ace pilot who really knows his plane.

The sea-plane, a Cessna 185, is a lightweight amphibian vehicle used

Above: *The sea-plane sequence provides a really original adventure section for* Licence to Kill. *Here the camera being used to film the action is located in the helicopter.*

Left: *Standing amongst the wreckage of the planes use for the action shots of* Licence to Kill *are two of the doctors.*

for transportation or pleasure. The pilot, Mark Juckett, usually flies people out to the off-shore oil rigs in South Louisiana and was delighted by the break in his routine as he prepared to fly on his first Bond movie. 'I'm used to having to work for a living,' he joked. 'My plane's never seen clear water before.'

PROFILE

Name: J.W. 'Corkey' Fornof

Bond history: *Octopussy* (AcroStar jet pilot), *Licence to Kill* (aerial co-ordinator)

Corkey Fornof is one of those characters who have lent their talents to many of the more recent Bond films. He is an aviation expert dealing with everything – and anything – aerial as far as stunts are concerned. A short, rotund man, he is quite unlike the popular idea of a daredevil pilot.

Corkey started out in the entertainment business as a test pilot, flying in air shows for some 23 years. He then graduated to TV commercials and bit parts in films, doing whatever airborne action the piece called for. Although he did some TV specials on aerobatics and sports spectaculars, he never really thought that

this would continue. In fact, he found he was more interested in his work as a test pilot. At first he just flew the stunts, then he started organizing it all and nowadays he is one of the most renowned aerial stunt co-ordinators in the movie business.

This is Corkey's third Bond film – it would have been his fourth had the waterfall necessary for an aerial stunt in *Moonraker* not dried up before they could shoot. His job entails planning the stunt, executing it, hiring the right people for it, getting all the necessary clearances and permits, and generally making sure it all works out smoothly.

In *Licence to Kill*, he is concerned with several sequences: a helicopter 'capturing' a small plane on its winch in the pre-title sequence; Bond water-skiing behind a sea-plane; and, most spectacularly, landing a crop-duster on top of a fast-moving truck. In this last stunt, Corkey decided to fly the plane himself.

Stunts like these are no strangers to Corkey – or to the Bond films. It was Corkey who flew the tiny, fold-away AcroStar jet in *Octopussy*, even looping the loop in a box canyon but that footage was not finally used. More recently, in Disney's *The Rescuers* (1977), he effected a dead engine landing with a British Freighter (similar to a DC10) from a mile-and-a-half away.

'The problem with stunts,' Corkey pronounced 'is that you're always in the firing line. If you do it, everyone says, "Gee that's great" while if it goes wrong they all say it couldn't be done anyway.'

Right: *The storyboard shows in detail the action and angle of the shots in a sequence. The section depicted here shows how Bond chases the plane on waterskis, climbs aboard the plane and tackles the pilot. The intercutting between Bond's progress and the scenes in the cockpit are a good guide to the likely final cut of the film.*

BOND GRADUALLY APPEARS ABOVE THE WATER ... THRU' SPRAY ...

BOND GRABS ONTO FLOAT AS IT CLEARS THE SURFACE TO BECOME AIRBORNE ...

CO-PILOT DRAWS REVOLVER AND MAKES FOR REAR DOOR ...

CO-PILOT FALLS FROM PLANE ...

DOLLAR BILLS FLY AROUND ... BOND BEATS PILOT SENSELESS ...

BOND GRABS CONTROLS AND FLIES PLANE ... PILOT UNCONCIOUS IN BROKEN SEAT ...

A DAY IN THE LIFE OF THE FIRST UNIT ON LOCATION

A typical day at Key West began early in the morning at the Coast Guard pier where breakfast was served. About 150 people (a reduced unit) waited patiently to be ferried in numerous boats out to the *Wavekrest* which was moored some miles away in a secluded cove. By speedboat the trip, which has to negotiate a series of treacherous sandbanks, takes under half an hour. By other means it can take much longer. On one memorable day, a cruise boat took three hours to navigate these waters. To save time, they tried to do the make-up on the way out but the sea was too rough, the make-up mirrors kept falling over and there was even the odd case of sea-sickness.

John Glen and the camera crew were the first to reach the *Wavekrest* and they settled down for a bout of early morning planning. John and Alec Mills, the director of photography, stalked around the practically empty boat, plotting camera positions and angles for the day's filming. 'On location,' Alec quipped, 'God lights the scene, I just help by filling in the shadows.'

As the rest of the crew gradually arrived and grabbed a ritual cup of coffee, the *Wavekrest* became a tiny island in the middle of nowhere. Other boats were constantly coming alongside bringing materials, equipment, people and endless supplies of ice and cold drinks. The boat became a busy hive of people as the crew moved around filming from place to place while the boat was returned to normal in their wake.

A small armada of boats, surrounded the *Wavekrest* – shuttles to Key West, camera boats, ferries to the second unit, press boats and many others. That particular morning, John and the camera crew went off in a flat camera boat to plan the morning's shots. It was the scene where, as Bond flies over the *Wavekrest*, he pushes the pilot out of the plane and into the water. The discussion was about possible angles, how low the plane needed to

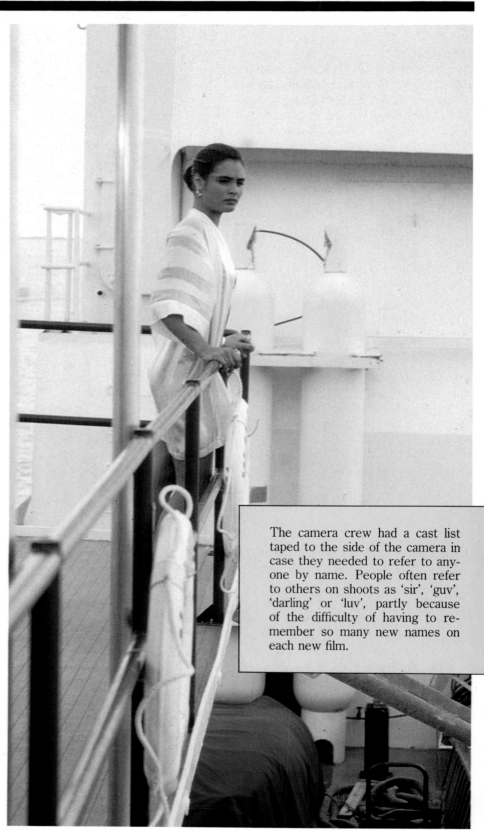

The camera crew had a cast list taped to the side of the camera in case they needed to refer to anyone by name. People often refer to others on shoots as 'sir', 'guv', 'darling' or 'luv', partly because of the difficulty of having to remember so many new names on each new film.

Above: *Lupe (Talisa Soto) is watching the action aboard the* Wavekrest. *Even filming on a boat moored an hour away from the mainland, Talisa maintains her glamorous image.*

fly, what lenses might be appropriate, how to make sure a bit of the *Wavekrest* was in frame, whether it mattered if the sun intruded and burned out the shot.

Michael Frift, the camera operator, described this process as picking the picture out of the director's brain. He spent 14 years as a focus puller, listening to operators, learning the different ways in which directors work. He finds John flexible, someone who is always willing to listen to the actors or the crew if they have ideas. This was his sixth Bond and he obviously enjoys his work on them.

Then there was a rehearsal to check the height of the plane, its angle of approach to the *Wavekrest* and the position of the camera boat. Two cameras were set to record the action – Michael was on the camera boat and Alec had a second camera on the *Wavekrest*. Michael was using a hand-held harness, a balanced contraption which allows the operator, with the aid of the grip, to lean over the edge of the boat in safety. Alec invented the device some 15 years ago and they have been using it ever since. This shot was being filmed at a slightly slower speed than normal, so that more of it was captured on film, allowing the action

to last just that crucial little bit longer.

The Bond crew are proud of their ability to work together. Having worked as a team on five Bonds over 10 years, they talked about the importance of knowing how everybody else on the crew works and how this facilitates easy communications in a crisis. That very day the stage was set for a convincing demonstration of this.

Above: *A typical scene from the filming days aboard the* Wavekrest. *Anthony Zerbe (playing Milton Krest), director John Glen and the camera crew are all waiting for the next shot.*
Below left: *Edward Tise, the sound recordist, was a new member of the team. Edward comes from a documentary background, having worked around the world on a variety of socio-political films.*

More recently, he moved into features, working on Stanley Kubrick's Full Metal Jacket *(1987). He not only recorded all the sound, meticulously cataloguing all the different noises that guns, bombs and grenades make, but also edited the sound himself.*

On Licence to Kill *his aim was to record as clean a soundtrack as possible, often in extremely difficult conditions – even the sound stages at Churubusco were not completely soundproofed.*

THE SHOOT

Location	No. of days
Main Unit	
Churubusco Studios	63
Mexico City and	
surrounds	9
Key West	20
Acapulco	6
Second Unit	
Key West	12
Mexicali	46
Other	2
Aerial Unit	19
Underwater Unit	32
Other Units	5

As the crew were preparing for a take, a cacophony of instructions suddenly burst over the walkie-talkies ... 'It's coming in,' one voice said; 'We're not ready, we're not turning,' another responded with panic; 'I can't hold it,' a third voice announced; 'Turn over,' someone else shouted. 'We can't, we haven't got a stop,' the camera crew replied.

A request for a rough translation elicited the information that John Richardson, holding the dummy pilot in the plane, was finding it too heavy to control and was going to have to drop it very soon. The dummy is operated by compressed air so that its legs can kick realistically during the fall. It weighs some 30kg (70 lb). John and Corkey Fornof in the plane were saying they needed to shoot at once. Meanwhile, the camera crew on the boat had not had their final instruction from Alec on the *Wavekrest* as to which stop they should set the camera at for the prevalent lighting conditions. But given the circumstances, they had to go ahead and shoot anyway. The team pulled together, the adrenalin flowed, every person automatically played their part and the shot was taken with little warning. But the result was exactly what they wanted – the cameras caught the fall of the

pilot into the water just as they had initially planned.

Then it was back to the boat and some more familiar and everyday images from the shoot. John Glen in a Texan hat and white suit, sitting on his director's chair, waiting patiently for the next shot, looking like a benevolent cowboy. When the waiting got too much he counted to ten or chatted about golf to the nearest available enthusiast. Finally he said 'Come on, boys and girls, let's get this one,' and things started to happen. But John is well aware that waiting is a necessary evil of any shoot. 'The responsibility for safety lies with the director,' he explained. 'If something changes after the rehearsal, then we have to start it all again in case something unexpected has been caused by the change.'

John may appear unhurried and unpressurized but on this shoot his job is a 24-hour one. While working with the main unit, he is also controlling three, maybe four, other units, having meetings or extended phone calls in the evening to discuss their progress and viewing rushes to move the editing forward. His experience as an editor is invaluable on the shoot. He can almost visualize the cut sequences in his head and

knows what material he needs from each unit to cover the scene.

Miguel Gil was brought in as the first assistant on this, his first Bond because he is bi-lingual in English and Spanish. He is a veteran of large-scale epic films, like *Nicholas and Alexandra* (1971), *Fire Walker*

Left: *Michael Frift, the camera operator, and the camera crew are lining up a shot.*

Right: *June Randall, the script supervisor, 'Cubby' Broccoli and John Glen pose for a shot between takes at the airstrip near Key West.*

Below right: *Sometimes the traditional methods are the best, particularly when the director needs to communicate with his crew.*

Chunky Huse, the grip, has worked with this camera crew on many films. His knowledge of the American system and its differences from the British is useful. In America, gripping covers a multitude of sins, from riggers to stand-bys. 'Nobody specializes,' he explained, 'every job nobody wants is grips.'

Left: *Getting a close-up of Bond water-skiing requires the camera boat to be alongside. It will produce a fast-moving action shot for the sequence.*

(1986) and *Omar Muktar* (1981) which found him filming for seven months in Libya. Miguel, who could always raise a smile with his slightly stilted, impatient English idioms, had the job of holding the unit together. In one shot, for instance, with seven extras on the boats and another six hanging over the side, Miguel could spot which one of them was missing. In many ways, he did John's yelling for him, trying to get things moving, allowing John to remain calm and eternally charming.

However inhospitable a location, June Randall, who was responsible for continuity, was always to be found sitting comfortably ensconced with her typewriter at her table.

During the day's filming, she carefully watched every shot and recorded both the action in front of the camera and the details behind camera – its position, what lenses were used, how much footage is shot and so on. It is her job to ensure that the continuity between scenes – and between units – is always correct. Timothy Dalton, she considers, is excellent at continuity. He would remind June, for instance, that his coat should be open, while she would remind him that his glass should be in his left hand.

Each day's filming produced about four hours of paperwork for June to do in the evening, filling in the continuity sheets, writing up the progress reports and creating what she called a 'storybook script' with polaroids of each scene attached to the appropriate place in the script. (The one she did for *Gandhi* (1982), she had bound in leather as a present for Sir Richard Attenborough.) 'This is a young person's job,' she commented about her workload. 'You need every bit of energy you can get.'

June referred to the camera crew as 'my boys'. She has watched every one of them grow up and rise through the ranks. She is used to being the only woman on the floor of the unit and recognizes no allowances are ever made for this – not even in the toilet arrangements. 'A good continuity girl,' she said 'will keep her head when all around her are losing theirs.'

Even when rain threatened and people and gear were moved under cover, the filming carried on because on such a tight schedule it could be a disaster to fall behind. But by mid-afternoon, the sea was too choppy to do the planned skiing stunt and anyway the seaplane, which is necessary for the action, had disappeared. So instead the sequence being filmed was one where Bond swims underwater to the *Sentinel*. It is packed with cocaine and Bond angrily splits all the containers open, spilling their contents into the sea. During the filming, one of the underwater crew did not surface at the command to 'cut'. Immediately several people dived in and pulled him to safety. He had got into one of

those underwater states when it is difficult to tell which way is up.

Then it rained properly, heavily, and the whole crew took shelter, either in the cabin with the camera gear or up on deck, huddling under the tiny bit of shelter afforded by a canopy.

Meanwhile Callum McDougal, the second assistant, was up in the bridge trying desperately to organize the next day's shoot. He was surrounded by telephones and radios, having several methods of communication at his disposal. A repeater radio linked him to the production office in Key West. Sea-to-land telephone connections are very expensive and used sparingly. It failed after two hours anyway, which put it out of action. He had ground-to-air communication to talk to the seaplane and boat-to-boat radios for coordinating all the boats in the vicinity. He also had a walkie-talkie to communicate with the unit itself.

Above: *Director John Glen.*

Whenever he started to speak on one radio, it blocked all the others out and since they were all going all the time, he rarely managed to finish a conversation. Somehow, though, everything got arranged and the day went smoothly.

Then at last, everyone moved to the shuttles to return to Key West. The previous night, four boats, including the pilot boat, had got stuck on sandbanks on their way back. They had been shooting late and in the rush to return in the dark, even the experienced Key West pilots ran aground. When another boat came to the rescue, the first priority was to protect all the film that had been shot that day. It could not be risked on a hand-to-hand transfer to the new boat. Eventually they found a solution – the stock was floated across to safety in one of the drinks coolers.

A DAY IN THE LIFE OF THE SECOND UNIT

INT. ARMOURED TRUCK — KILLIFER WITH SHOTGUN AND DRIVER —

DRIVERS POV FROM ADJOINING TRUCK —

KILLIFER PULLS ON STEERING WHEEL —

VAN SMASHES THRU' BARRIER —

Production Office: 422 Fleming St., Key West - Florida 33040/Tel.: (305) 292-7600

CINEMA CONSULTANTS, Inc.
"LICENSE REVOKED"
2nd Unit CALL SHEET

PRODUCERS: A. R. BROCCOLI / MICHAEL WILSON   **Call Sheet No. 4**

DIRECTOR: ARTHUR WOOSTER   **DATE:** THURSDAY – 4th August 1988

LOCATION: 1) Old 7-Mile Bridge, Marathon 2) Pigeon Island (If not shot.)

UNIT CALL: 07.00am Lv Hotels / 08.00am On Location

SETS:
1) EXT. Armoured Convoy on Bridge (Aerial) - If not shot.
2) EXT. Armoured Convoy on Bridge (Run-bys)
3) INT. ARMOURED VAN

SC. NOS:
1) 45pt. 47pt. Day. S/B 1. 1A.
2) 45pt. 47pt. Day. 49. 51pt. Day. S/B 7. 8. 9.
3) 48. 50. Day. S/B 2. 3. 4. 5. 6.

ARTISTE	CHARACTER	P/UP	M-UP/HAIR	ON SET
EVERETT McGILL	Killifer	07.00	08.00	Line-Up
Stunts:				
CHICK BERNHARDT	Marshall Driver	-		
TOM BAHR	Marshall	-	07.30	08.30
ALEX EDLIN	Marshall	-		09.00 on location
		-		09.00 on location
Doubles:				
BRUNO WUETHRICH	Killifer	07.00	-	08.00 on location
MICH MICHELSON	Marshall (Driver)	07.00		08.00 on location
Action Helicopter Pilot:				
RANDY MEADE	Coast Guard Pilot	-	-	08.00 on location
Crowd:				
8 x MEN/WOMEN	Drivers (4 w/cars)	-	-	
4 X MEN	Marshalls		08.00	
20 x MEN	Security Guards	07.00	08.00	when ready
2 x MEN	Motorcycle Police	07.00	08.00	
1 x MAN	Co-Pilot (Via Coast Guard)	07.00	08.00	
1 x MAN	Rescuers			
1 x MAN	Diver (via Coast Guard)	07.00	08.00	08.00 on location
3 x MEN	Press	07.00		
2 x MEN	Security Guards (at Gate)	07.00	08.00	
		07.00	08.00	
Action Plane:				
COASTGUARD HELICOPTER	(Lift off Key West)	07.45		08.00 on location
Action Vehicles:				
ARMOURED CAR				
2 x RIOT VANS				08.00 on location
2 x MARSHALL VANS				08.00 on location
2 x MOTORBIKES				08.00 on location
7 x CARS (VIA CROWD)				08.00 on location
Camera Crane:				08.00 on location
Tulip crane required				
Facility Boats:				
2 x PATROL BOATS				08.00 on location
2 x SAFETY BOATS (with 2 x divers)				
1 x SPECIAL EFFECTS BOAT (with divers)				08.00 on location
1 x CAMERA BOAT/PONTOON				08.00 on location
				08.00 on location
				08.00 on location

*For the day's action filming, the second unit need the storyboard (**above left**) and the call sheet (**above right**). Between them it says everything they need to know. The storyboard itemises the shots while the call sheet lists who and what need to be where and when. The day's filming, shown in the storyboard, is about Sanchez' escape from the armoured truck with the aid of the double-crossing DEA agent, Killifer.*

The Bond second unit is special. It is the unit that stages all the action sequences, films all the backgrounds that do not need the star actors and generally sweeps up after the main unit, catching whatever it might have missed. It is a small, tight-knit unit, used to the complexities of action filming. John Glen made his name in the Bond series as the second unit director of *On Her Majesty's Secret Service* and subsequent Bond films.

He became the director of the series with *For Your Eyes Only* but his experience with action sequences remains an invaluable asset. He works on them from the beginning, visualizing how they can be filmed, planning the storyboards and organizing the shooting. Then Arthur Wooster comes in as director of the second unit and puts it all into practice.

A number of the crew have worked with Arthur on several occasions – including four or five Bonds – and they all obviously like and respect each other. They have a particular fondness for Arthur. 'I've never met anyone with as much nerve as Arthur. He would never ask the crew to do what he wouldn't do himself,' said Ken Atherfold, the unit grip. It leads to a very relaxed atmosphere, extremely important when undertaking the kind of detailed, tricky action shots that are the second unit's speciality.

At Key West the day started for the crew at seven o'clock in the morning. As they assembled outside the hotel, they met the first unit returning from the night shoot, since at that time as one crew was finishing the other would be starting work. Pleasantries were ritually exchanged – 'Did you get that shot?' 'How did it look?' 'Can we have the Tulip crane next Friday?' and so on. It was an hour's drive to the location – the stunning Seven Mile Bridge which connects two of the Florida keys. (The bridge is, in fact, only 10.9 km, 6.8 miles, long.)

On the way, Sue, the continuity girl, mentioned her experience of the previous evening. She had been relaxing with a drink in the hotel pool, when she saw the *Wavekrest* out at sea being filmed at night by the main unit. She noticed immediately that it was flying two flags whereas previously, in the second unit's hands, it had been flying only one. A quick call to the set and the matter was put to rights.

At the location Arthur, proudly sporting his new cap, given to him by the Sheriff's Department of Munroe County, and Terry Madden, the first assistant, checked that everything was in order while the rest of the crew settled down to breakfast – eggs, toast, bacon or burritos. (After three weeks in Mexico, few of the crew were willing to try the burritos).

The day's filming was in two parts. In the morning there were the 'run-by' shots of the armoured truck that is taking Sanchez to jail. Inside the truck, Killifer has to cosh the other guard with a rifle butt. The afternoon was set to be more spectacular – the truck would be filmed going over

the edge of the bridge into the water below, taking its occupants with it. Both scenes are part of the sequence in which Sanchez escapes from captivity.

Two discussions began immediately: how to make the coshing look effective in the first sequence and how high the tide needed to be for the second sequence if the truck was not going to get stuck in the sands below. While these points were being debated, the crew moved to the bridge itself, to start preparing

Right: *Everett McGill plays Killifer, the DEA agent whose job is to deliver Sanchez safely to the authorities – but money speaks louder than duty.*

Below: *The huddle before the action as Arthur Wooster explains the reactions he wants when the armoured truck crashes over the side of the bridge.*

Above: *A shot from the day's filming when the SWAT team watch helplessly as the armoured truck falls into the water below.*

Below: *George Whitear has been the stills photographer on the Bond second unit for many years. Despite being a grandfather, he is at home with the arduous rigours of action shooting.*

'How comes the art department and special effects get all the sexy cars?' said Arthur Wooster, jealously one day.

the truck for the shot. Terry Madden was responsible for making sure everything was running smoothly and was ready for the director when he wanted it. Terry had been the second assistant on the main unit before he was 'demoted' to be first assistant on the second. He kept up a relaxed, cheery chatter throughout the day, fending off each new crisis with consummate ease.

Ken Atherfold was in charge of building the rig – a platform on the front of the truck which allowed the cameraman to film through the windscreen while the truck was moving. Ken has worked on four Bond films and has earned the nickname of 'Mister Magic' from the crew for his imaginative rigs which have allowed the second unit to shoot in the tightest of spots. Ken used to own Grip House in London, a company which supplied gripping gear (cranes, dollies, tracks and other equipment needed to allow the camera to move). While he was there, he helped to design the Python – a remote-control crane that was used, for instance, for filming actually among the horses for the recreation of the Grand National for *Champions* (1985).

For Bond, he has created rigs on

the Eiffel Tower and on the San Francisco Bridge (both for *A View to a Kill*), and in the back of a Hercules plane (*The Living Daylights*). His most challenging venture involved rigging two cameras together so that Arthur could operate them both, standing below an overhang of ice for the pre-title sequence, filmed in Iceland, of *A View to a Kill*. Ken's rigs are usually simple in design without any of the complicated electronics that abound in the industry. As Arthur said 'it is important to keep things simple. The more complex things go wrong more easily'.

While the truck was being rigged, Arthur was discussing blood. Di Holt (make-up) and Rodney Pincott (props) had been experimenting with blood capsules to make the guard's injury look serious. But Arthur was not happy – he wanted the effect to look very real. Di had various kinds of blood in her armoury – caked blood, more liquid kinds, frothy blood – and she mixed different

types together until she got exactly what she wanted. Meanwhile Rodney fiddled with the capsules, taping them to the end of Killifer's rifle, finding the right position for the impact.

Then everyone settled down to wait, while the truck was prepared. Second units are sometimes known as 'action units' but the name is something of a misnomer as much of the shoot involves hanging around and waiting … waiting for the rig, waiting for the lights, waiting for radio contacts to be set up, waiting for the sun to pass a cloud, just generally waiting. Arthur finds this the hardest thing to cope with on the shoot but looking at his calm, dapper appearance, you would never ever know it.

The truck made things particularly difficult on the Seven Mile Bridge. In fact, there were two armoured trucks: a standard one for run-bys and one specially fitted with remote control for the crash. The standard one often didn't work. In the course

of three days, it had broken down several times, the fan belt and the transmission being largely responsible. Finally with the truck working, the rig in place, the blood right, the continuity Polaroids from the main unit checked to ensure that everything matched with what they had shot, the lights placed and the actors in position, it was time to start filming.

On a section of the old road bridge that runs to Pigeon Key, an island in the middle of the bridge, the truck moved off, stopping for adjustments between takes. At the end of the road, the truck had to turn round and the steering lock promptly jammed, rendering the truck once again immobile. The crew settled down for another long wait. 'It's always like this,' said Arthur philosophically.

At times like these, everybody remains amazingly calm, waiting patiently for things to happen. While some people spotted exotic fish like stingrays swimming below the bridge, most regaled each other with endless chat about other shoots. 'Do you remember when...', 'When I was on...' and so on. Arthur, Terry and Malcolm MacIntosh, the camera operator, discussed other Bond shoots. There was the time in Iceland (in *A View to a Kill*) when they were filming on the ice. They turned back as the film stock ran out just in time to avoid a major ice-flow crash.

Or the time, on the same shoot, when they were sitting having lunch on an iceberg and somebody realized they were getting a little wet. The iceberg was slowly turning over. They all promptly leapt off, leaving the camera gear to fend for itself. Or filming from the back of the Hecules plane (in *The Living Daylights*) above the Atlas mountains, when Arthur wanted the plane to fly lower and even the crew of the plane were begging the pilot to go higher.

Eventually, the truck was ready again, the shot was taken and it was time for a break. Lunch was held in a marquee that provided a welcome respite from the heat. Standing on the bridge, there is no shade and in Florida it is even worse in the afternoon, when by rights the sun should be slowly sinking. But there, it goes on heating up the atmosphere relentlessly until four or five. There is little relief then, even in the shade. The crew used towels constantly refreshed in Sea Breeze, a magic liquid that somehow cools the body down.

Then it was time to move back to the bridge to begin to set up the afternoon's stunt. John Richardson and his special effects department had already installed a remote control device, which they built and tested at Key West, into the truck. It had a transmitter and receiver similar to the type used in the top range of kids' models. While John had often used remote control devices before, he had never driven a radio-controlled, full-size vehicle and he was understandably nervous.

Everything had been carefully prepared. Boards had been specially built so that the truck could drive on a level with the road, leaving it without a kerb, and a section of the railing has been replaced by wood. The most difficult thing to do was to drive the vehicle, using the remote control, in a straight line, at the right speed and then turn it at exactly the right time and place for it to crash over the edge.

As they set it up, John realized he had to make some adjustments. The army truck following the armoured vehicle was causing too much static for the vehicle to be controlled from behind as planned,

Left: *The convoy accompanying Sanchez imprisoned in the armoured truck drives along the Seven Mile Bridge.*

Below: *A close-up (seen in the storyboard on the previous page) of Killifer coshing the guard.*

On this particular morning, the crew woke up to find there was no water anywhere on the island. This led to an interesting new experience for many: washing in Perrier, from their room bars. The clearer-thinking remembered the hotel swimming-pool and found a more refreshing way to wake up.

Above: *Towards the end of the day's filming, the armoured car finally performed its spectacular dive over the edge of the bridge.*

so John had to guide the vehicle from the front – an even more difficult proposition. They began to practise driving, John working the remote controls and an assistant in the truck, ready to slam on the brakes if anything went wrong. ('I know it's safe, but I keep looking down to check that the brake is still there –just in case,' he commented drily as the truck stopped just short of the drop.) But they got the angle right first time and then it was just a question of speeding it up. 'It looks as if you've been practising all night,' I told John. 'I have,' he responded, 'in my bed.'

They only wanted to have to do this shot once, so three cameras were used to record the action from different angles. Arthur argued that it was not worth doing complicated tracking shots as director John Glen usually cuts his scenes fast and anything complex would land on the cutting-room floor.

The main camera was on the road, in the path of the truck, where it would drive if it were not going off over the edge. For safety's sake, a platform had been built for Malcolm MacIntosh at the side of the bridge out of harm's way and his camera was on remote control. This was another of the camera crew's simple set ups. The camera was fixed to any camera head and linked by cables to a video screen, where Malcolm could operate the controls. The other two cameras were at the foot of a bank, poised to capture the truck going over the bridge and hitting the water – one filming wide and the other in close-up. The stunt was to be filmed at a slightly slower speed than normal to make the action last that little bit longer.

Then the waiting began in earnest. There were extras to key in – the troops who run to the edge of the bridge to see what has happened to the truck. A helicopter had to be given air clearance, then find its position and angle of approach to the armoured convoy. Special effects were sawing through the wooden railings to make sure the truck could easily crash through them. Numerous boats patrolled the water, stopping any yachts from straying into

the area. Divers were at the ready in case of problems. And, of course, the crew were waiting for the tide to be just right.

George Whitear, the stills photographer, was also at the ready. On a unit like this he has a difficult job. He has to find a position where he can capture the action in a way that's worth having, but not interfere with the filming itself. 'You're Cinderella,' he explained 'but on this unit, if it's possible to get the photo, these guys will make sure I got it. And that goes from the director to any of the crew.' For this shot, George has three cameras poised. One is on remote, one is in his hands and he has pressed Di from the make-up department into service to take care of the other.

More and more people were arriving. The key people from the production office showed up to watch the fun and holidaymakers converged on foot or by boat to enjoy the spectacle. And it was getting hotter by the minute.

Finally a production assistant warned the crowd to be quiet during the shot and pleaded for no cheering when the truck goes over as the cameras would still be turning. This was particularly hard on the crew who were, by then, so fed up with the truck that they were overjoyed to finally see the back of it.

The stunt happened and everything looked fine. A few pick-up shots remained and then it was back to the hotel. But the day was not over yet. For Sue, in charge of continuity, it was back to her room to type up the day's continuity sheets and progress report; for Marcia, the second assistant, it was back to the production office to finalize the details of the next day's shoot; for Arthur, it was off to the main unit to discuss the day's work with John Glen. The rest of the crew fell gratefully into a shower, exhausted after another day's work.

PROFILE

Name: Arthur Wooster

Bond history: *For Your Eyes Only* (second unit director and cameraman), *Octopussy* (second unit director and cameraman), *A View to a Kill* (second unit director and cameraman), *The Living Daylights* (second unit director and cameraman), *Licence to Kill* (second unit director and cameraman).

Arthur Wooster, the chirpy second unit director and cameraman, started in the film industry as a clapper boy at Pinewood on Humphrey Jennings' *The Cumberland Story* (1947). He left Pinewood to set up his own independent production company, Film Partnership, which specialized in documentaries and commercials. The company was chaired by the English television presenter Richard Dimbleby. For seven years Arthur filmed around the world and then moved into features, slowly working his way up through the grades – clapper loader, focus puller, operator – until he became a director of photography.

He was in America, shooting John Schlesinger's *Honky Tonk Freeway* (1981) when John Glen was offered the chance to direct his first Bond, *For Your Eyes Only*. John rang Arthur up and asked him if he would be interested in the second unit, both as director and cameraman. They had known each other from Arthur's Film Partnership days when John had done some editing for them but they had not seen each other since. Now, of course, they work together very closely, planning the shooting of the action sequences and consulting each other at the end of each day's filming.

Arthur is the kind of director who always wants to take the filming just that little bit further to get an exciting edge to the action sequences but he is experienced enough to know when he can only sit and wait. 'You can't push on this sort of shoot,' he explained. 'We have to wait until special effects or stunts are ready, otherwise it's dangerous.'

As Alec Mills, the director of photography, put it, 'He's a great bundle of enthusiasm,' on the set, eagerly explaining what he wants done, impatiently checking the progress of his different set-ups, philosophically accepting all the myriad problems and delays that beset the unit and happily chatting away about his past experiences to anyone free to listen.

Arthur uses several of the Bond team – Malcolm MacIntosh, the camera operator, Michael Evans, the focus puller, and Ken Atherfold, the grip – on his other films, when he is usually the director of photography. Consequently, they all work together smoothly and easily. Most recently, just before *Licence to Kill*, he completed a stint in the Philippines, shooting *Return from the River Kwai* (1989). When this Bond film is finished, Arthur will immediately begin another movie; his skills are always in demand and he rarely stops working.

Left: *Arther Wooster prepares for a helicopter shot – using it to film in.*

Below: *The second and third camera positions for the truck's fall.*

Above: *The second unit camera crew show off their camera mounted on 'bunjies' for the flying shots.*

Below: *John Richardson, the special effects supervisor, plays with his remote-controlled truck.*

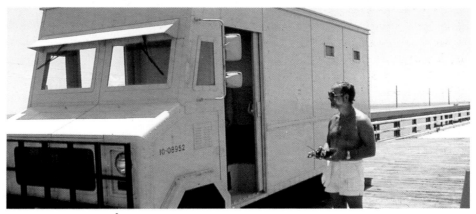

MEXICO CITY AND ENVIRONS

THE CASINO ESPAGNOL

When Bond decides to meet Sanchez, he goes to his casino in Isthmus City, spends a lot of money at the gaming tables and gets himself invited upstairs to meet the boss. Gambling is now illegal in Mexico and so an appropriate alternative location had to be found. The Casino Espagnol was, in its heyday, a plush casino patronized by the rich and famous of Mexico City. Today it is a fairly elite club for the Spanish community in Mexico – including well-respected people like Benito Juarez' grandson, factory owners and brewery magnates – who meet there to talk or play billiards, cards, chess or dominoes. It is owned by its 250 members and boasts a restaurant, a library and a bar.

The manager, Miguel Hidalgo Perez, who has been at the Casino Espagnol for 40 years, is from the same family as the famous Mexican President Miguel Hidalgo. He is justifiably proud of the club and its associations. A lot of films are made there, in order to raise the money needed to preserve the very beautiful old building. They are especially delighted to play host to *Licence to Kill* because its casino connections remind them of their own more glorious past when Porfirio Diaz came here to celebrate Mexico's independence.

Having found the location, the next problem was to find the croupiers, waiters and glamorous clientele who might frequent such a place.

Below: *The Casino Espagnol in Mexico City provided an elegant location for Sanchez' casino.*

Above: *John Glen directs Carey Lowell and Timothy Dalton in the scene at the casino.*

Callum McDougal, the second assistant, who is responsible, among other things, for finding extras, could only come up with one actor in Mexico City who had experience as a croupier. But he had very long hair and refused to have it cut for the film. The next closest to a card dealer that Callum could find was a magician. In the end, Poulson Dice, the company who supplied the gaming equpiment, which itself had to be brought in from Las Vegas, used their own professional croupiers.

The director of the company, his wife and some of their friends also came to Mexico City – to be extras in the scene.

Finding competent waiters was also difficult. The barman from the Crowne Plaza hotel (where many of the crew stayed) was brought in to show other extras how to do things properly. The irony here was that the crew had themselves previously had to teach him how to mix Bond's famous Vodka Martini.

Glamorous girls were less of a problem and the scene was liberally sprinkled with the kind of beauties that always grace a Bond film. Some came from model agencies in Mexico City; others included the star of a soap opera, the hostess of a TV aerobics show and several competition winners. Lucinda Dunn from Adelaide won an Australian Bond girl contest and found herself overseas for the first time in her life. She wore a $2,000 Neiman Marcus designer dress of salmon and silver-lurex, originally intended for Pam.

Below: *Loti (Diana Lee Hsu) is a Hong Kong narcotics agent.*

THE MAIN POST OFFICE

Built in the 1930s in an unusual combination of black metal, gilt and marble, Mexico City's central Post Office is an exceptionally attractive building dominated by an angular grand staircase with four interlocking flights. It was designed by Adamo Boari, who was also the architect of the famous Palacio de las Bellas Artes, also in Mexico City. It is, according to Joel Agula, who is proud to be its administrator, one of the biggest and most beautiful post offices in the world. In *Licence to Kill*, it becomes the Banco de Isthmus, the Isthmus City bank through which Sanchez launders his money.

The Post Office is a major centre for rare stamps and collectors converge on it from all over the world. *Licence to Kill* was filmed there while the public were still using the building and the administrator had the foresight to put on extra staff to handle the complaints. Filming, nevertheless, proceeded smoothly, apart from one small incident. Phil Kohler, the location manager, had asked for one of the magnificent brass revolving doors to be cleaned but unfortunately the wrong one was given the treatment. It all had to be done again, at six o'clock in the morning, before the crew arrived and the day's filming began.

At lunchtime, it was decided that, since the crew were in the Post Office for the day, they might as well film the scene set in the bank's trading room there as well. The art department had to drop everything, calling all hands on deck, to bring in the desks, monitors, computers and typewriters and to change all the Post Office notice boards, to turn it into the trading room. They had about two hours to put it all together. Disaster nearly struck when the lorry containing all the desks got lost en route but some Victorian replacements were found in a back room of the Post Office and used instead.

Below: *The Isthmus City Bank is Sanchez' main channel for laundering money. It was filmed in the main Post Office in Mexico City and Sanchez (Robert Davi) can be seen in this shot with Truman-Lodge (Anthony Starke), his financial advisor, and Kwang (Cary-Hiroyuki Tagawa) who Sanchez believes to be a potential colleague in the Far East.*

Right: *This elaborate double staircase is the central feature of the Post Office.*

GRAN HOTEL 'CIUDAD DE MEXICO'

Located on one side of the Zocolo (Plaza de la Constitucion), the famous central square of Mexico City, which houses the National Palace and the Cathedral, is another beautiful Mexican building, the Gran Hotel 'Ciudad de Mexico'. Built in 1895 as a private house, it became a shop and finally a hotel in 1968. The hotel's imposing Art Nouveau foyer, with its gilt open lift, reminiscent of a bird cage, and its colourful French stained-glass ceiling became the lobby of the El Presidente Hotel in Isthmus City. The crew also filmed in the kitchen, corridors and lift.

Despite the fact that films are regularly shot in the hotel, the receptionists went into a flurry of excitement about Timothy Dalton filming there.

> Bancomer, one of the largest banks in Mexico, refused the unit permission to film there because they were worried that their shareholders would not like the image of their bank being used, albeit fictionally, to launder money.

Above: *This shot of Bond and Pam shows the beautiful art nouveau lift of the Gran hotel, Ciudad de Mexico.*

EL TEATRO DE LA CIUDAD

El Teatro de la Ciudad, Mexico City's theatre of traditional music and dancing, was used for the exterior shots of Sanchez office. One scene was shot in the theatre itself, and a replica was built in the studio for the interiors and the difficult scene where Bond climbs up the outside and blows a hole in the facade of the building.

The theatre was built in 1912. It seats some 1750 people but survives only with the help of a state subsidy, so playing host to a film company obviously helps the theatre financially. The day of the shoot looked as if it were going to be another of those days when everything went wrong but it all turned out well in the end.

The streets around the theatre had to be closed for filming but the Governor of the State of Nayarit and assorted important politicians and officials were due there for a charity programme of dancing and music in aid of the victims of a flood in Nayarit. The unit had to suspend operations while the performance was in progress. At one point the unit thought they would not be able to film at all until the event was over, which would have meant starting the shoot at 11 o'clock at night. But they managed it on schedule in the end. The major problem was that a news crew from Channel 11 was covering the Governor's visit. They not only parked their vehicles in the middle of the Bond film set but also placed all their cables, right in shot, over the door that the Bond unit were filming on.

Meanwhile Callum McDougal was having a different problem. Twenty soldiers had been pre-fitted in tight military costumes so there would be no difficulties over uniform on the shoot itself. Not only did they turn up half an hour late, but twenty entirely different people arrived for the filming. The preparation had all been in vain. Incidents like these were a regular part of filming in Mexico City.

Filming in these central locations did have its bonuses, however.

Wherever a film crew is working at least twenty – and often as many as thirty – large vans, trailers and wagons, carrying equipment, costumes and people are needed. As Arthur Dunn, the transport manager, explained, parking and traffic problems in Central London make this a logistic impossibility but the police in Mexico City are extremely co-operative and arrange the facilities that are needed.

BIBLIOTECA DE LA BANCO DE MEXICO

The exterior of El Presidente Hotel was filmed outside the Biblioteca de la Banco de Mexico, just one block away from the main Post Office in the centre of the city. The Bank of Mexico was the first bank to be established in Mexico in 1925 and its library, housed in this imposing building, was set up in 1984.

Even this small scene required a lot of attention to detail. To turn the library into an Isthmus City hotel, the building was decorated with flags, flowers, brass plates and special window boxes. Posters of the President were hung in the street. Cars with Isthmus City number plates were created and, perhaps most importantly for the Mexicans the gutters were mended.

Left: *This sequence, filmed outside El Teatro del Ciudad, which features a television reporter commenting on political life in Isthmus City, has had to be dropped from the film.*
Below left: *The El Teatro del Ciudad was used for the exterior of Sanchez' office and casino complex and featuring particularly in the scene where James Bond blows out the windows of the office.*

Above: *Frank Elliott, the focus puller of the camera crew, checks the lens while the scene outside El Teatro de la Ciudad, involving Timothy Dalton and Carey Lowell, is prepared.*

Below: *Q (Desmond Llewelyn) dons an unusual disguise. Going somewhat down in the world, he has become Bond's chauffeur.*

CENTRO CEREMONIAL OTOMI, TEMOAYA NEAR TOLUCA

It was difficult to find a location for the OMI Institute, the centre for which Joe Butcher makes televised appeals. The University had turned the unit down and various other possibilities had fallen through. Then, when John Glen and others were on a recce, they heard about a bizarre, ceremonial site for the Otomi people near Toluca. Even with a guide they had trouble finding it. They wandered around the area for hours before John Glen saw some unusual-shaped buildings in the distance and they headed for them. The shapes – cones – provided inspiration for the film and gave rise to the notion of 'cone power' which Butcher promotes.

It is a strange monumental place, built in 1980 as 'a meeting of philo-sophical, anthropological, educational, architectural, cultural and societal inspiration,' according to a plaque on one of its walls. Constructed of pinky grey stone, using totem pole and tent shapes, it is a modernist construction clearly inspired by traditional themes. A casual visitor could be forgiven, however, for thinking that the place was one of the wilder flights of fantasy of the Seventies' Bond films. The place was built as part of the movement to fulfil the aspirations of Mexico's indigenous cultures and the Otomi people, natives of that part of Mexico, gather there once a year. The rest of the time, which included the duration of the filming, it is deserted. It had to be the weirdest and most exotic location of the film.

Above: *A helicopter lands at the OMI seeking access to Sanchez' underground facilities. The OMI, a research institute for Joe Butcher's cone power organisation is ideal cover for Sanchez' drug trade. The Otomi ceremonial site at Toluca provided a very surreal and typical Bond setting.*

Left: *Truman-Lodge, running from the inevitable explosion that follows 007's discovery of the real purpose of the site.*

Right: *Pam, determined to infiltrate the OMI and help Bond, pretends to be infatuated with Butcher.*

ACAPULCO

Towards the end of the shoot, the unit went on location to Acapulco –the famous Mexican sun and sea resort – for a week. The production offices and many of the cast and crew were housed in one of the famous luxury hotels there. The weather was warm and sunny but by the end of the week, many people were homesick for Mexico City.

They had gone to Acapulco to find one special location. For Sanchez' house, director John Glen and production designer Peter Lamont wanted something different, somewhere that exuded wealth. 'We went to this fantastic home in Acapulco,' Peter said. The house, worth $32 million, had never been filmed in before but 'through the good offices of 'Cubby' and Dana, his wife, who have known the owners for many, many years, we were allowed to film there'. The crew were asked to wear soft-soled shoes during filming and not to smoke to avoid damaging any of the contents. The house was lent as a personal favour to 'Cubby' who made a handsome donation to a charity of the owner's choice to say thank you.

The house is built on four levels on the side of a cliff overlooking Acapulco Bay. 'It's not a normal type of house,' Peter Lamont enthused. 'The living-room is just huge and the finishes are incredible. So, in the story, Bond wakes up in this fantastic place, comes out on to a terrace where there is a camel train all in alabaster, then he comes downstairs into this enormous living-room.' The only part of the sequence that could not be shot there was the scene in Bond's bedroom because the guest rooms are furnished with art treasures which could easily be damaged. Bond's bedroom had to be constructed at the studios. 'Our bedroom has to echo what's in that house,' said Peter.

Towards the end of the movie, Bond sees Pam leaving the house and has to reach her quickly to stop her. The day before the filming was due to take place, John Glen realized that the special geography of the building meant that Bond could actually jump from one of the terraces into the swimming pool. It makes a great ending to *Licence to Kill*.

Above: *Acapulco is still one of the pleasure-seeking capitals of the world.*

Left: *Lupe is seen here at Sanchez' luxurious mansion.*

Right: *Bond grapples with two of Krest's divers while escaping from the* Wavekrest.

Below: *The* Shark Hunter *which is used in Sanchez' escape from prison and to track down Bond while he is trying to evade capture by Milton Krest and his men.*

CANCUN

The underwater sequences of *Licence to Kill* were shot at the Isla Mujeres (which in English means, the Island of Women) near the resort of Cancun on the Caribbean coast of Mexico. The shooting was supervised by Nicole Colin and Tony Broccoli with Ramon Bravo, one of the world's leading underwater photographers, directing the sequence. Ramon is also the author of seven bestselling Mexican novels.

Much of the underwater filming involving two of the *J. W. Powell*'s submersibles. The *Reef Hunter*, called the *Sentinel* in the film, looking like a large silver-grey bubble, and the sleek, bright yellow *Shark Hunter* are used in *Licence to Kill*. The *Reef Hunter* is a remote-controlled sub while the *Shark Hunter* is a two-man submersible, both of which run along the bottom of the sea at speeds of up to 3 knots (nautical miles per hour). The *Reef Hunter* is now no longer in use but the *Shark Hunter* is a useful vehicle. It is a 'wet' vehicle which means it fills up with water as it submerges and Scuba diving gear has to be worn. Pressure is equalized, inside and out, so it can go as deep as the diving gear allows. The advantage is that it doesn't use so much air as the occupants do not have to kick about or breathe so hard, and they can, of course, cover a lot more ground than a diver on his own.

The *Reef Hunter* was built in 1970, designed by Mr Perry's son. It has been used for looking for dead bodies under the sea by the Florida Sheriff's Department. It is a little harder to manouevre than the *Shark Hunter*. In the film, the *Sentinel* is used for transporting cocaine.

The *Shark Hunter*, built in 1975, was designed for Mr Perry himself, just for fun. It has been used in a lot of movies, including one or two Bonds. Just recently Perry Oceanographics have begun to market them, selling primarily to yacht owners who use them as toys to look, for instance, at underwater life in the Bahamas. Three weeks after the filming ended, Cancun was devastated by the Mexican hurricane.

MEXICALI

Facts and figures on the Mexicali shoot

7 week shoot

220 storyboard shots

120×400 ft rolls of film=48,000 ft

sequence will last between 11 and 14 minutes

shooting under 10 seconds a day

The dramatic car chase has long been an essential ingredient of any Bond movie. In the past, everything from Aston Martins to Citroen 2CVs has been used in exciting chase sequences. *Licence to Kill* adds a new dimension to the tradition when five giant tankers race across mountain roads with a lightweight plane used as a crop-duster, a pick-up truck, a jeep and a Maserati getting in on the action.

The setting for the filming of this climactic sequence is an irredeemably inhospitable landscape in the far north of Mexico. An hour's drive from Mexicali (a typical border town), there is a barren desert wasteland inhabited by little except tarantulas, snakes and scorpions. It is said to be one of the hottest places in the world where the temperatures are regularly about 120 F and have been known to reach 128 F. Director John Glen found the location while driving from Tijuana to Mexicali looking for likely places. Later, exploring the area from the air, they found the exact spots they wanted.

Rising menacingly above the desert is a winding mountain pass called the Rumorosa meaning 'rumours on the wind' after the cold winds that whistle through the area. It has been declared a black spot by the Red Cross. Crosses and abandoned, burnt-out vehicles litter the side of the road where drivers have gone over the edge and been killed.

Accidents were witnessed daily by the crew as they drove up the mountain to film on an abandoned road that wound around the top. On one occasion, the unit's fire brigade and ambulance went off to help a man whose two young kids were trapped in their car. They eventually emerged unscathed. The crew, however, managed to avoid injury until the last week when one of the French drivers found himself confronted by two lorries on his way down the mountain. He crashed into the side, wrote his tanker off and ended up in hospital with broken ribs.

Everything needed for filming in Mexicali, from typewriters to the tankers, had to be brought in specially. In this difficult terrain, the second unit even had to build their

own roads, bulldozing the land, digging out old concrete telegraph posts, clearing rocks and bushes, levelling the ground, importing sand from neighbouring areas to match other locations, making fibre glass rocks to dress the scenes and sand pits for the stunt men to dive into, and generally creating the terrain necessary for the shoot, without it looking like an obvious film set. Dennis Bosher, the art director, and Rodney Pincott, the stand-by prop, could be seen at any time digging away with their band of young Mexicans, keeping just one step ahead of the unit.

Working in these desert conditions created its own problems. At one time or another everything that could go wrong did – every vehicle took its turn to break down, every small thing needed for filming was difficult to find. As Crispin Reece, the production manager in Mexicali, put it, 'The primitiveness of this area of Mexico has to be experienced

Below: *In the rugged surrounds of the Rumorosa pass near Mexicali, the crew set up the shot of the final confrontation between Bond and Sanchez.*

Left: *The magnificent scenery of the Rumorosa pass provides the backdrop for the final climactic chase of the film.*
Below: *Edward Tise, the sound mixer, not only captured the sound accompanying the action, he also spent a lot of time recording 'wild tracks' which, when added to the soundtrack, will capture the flavour and atmosphere of the region.*

to be understood.'

Some problems were more spectacular. There was the time when a French driver, Gilbert Bataille, the only person who could drive the tanker on its side wheels, disappeared en route from Paris to Mexicali. He had apparently arrived in Mexico City but he checked out of his hotel, without money or credit cards, without any Spanish or English (and, according to Rémy Julienne, the stunt driver co-ordinator, without much French either), and vanished for a crucial 36 hours.

Another time a load of felt, specially purchased for simulating burning roads, mysteriously went up in flames overnight; or when a camera tilted off the back of the camera car, dragged along the ground and was seriously damaged. These incidents were just some of the tremendous difficulties that the crew faced to film this sequence.

Sometimes things went unexpectedly well, other times they went wrong. There was the day when a tanker was due to topple sideways off the road, rolling over and over down a specially prepared slipway. The tanker came off the road at the wrong point and only one of the three cameras poised to film the action captured it. Or another time, when two tankers collided, one accidentally hit the rock face at the side of the road, its front fell off spectacularly and that scene is now part of the movie. But this happy accident meant a close-up of an unplanned shot then had to be taken and matched with the previous action.

The filming involved a massive transport problem, with camera vehicles, passenger cars, action vehicles and water tankers all manoeuvering around the narrow, rocky roads to get in place for the next shot. With instructions being relayed in three languages – French, English and Spanish – the complexity of even the simplest operation was evident.

'It's like an army operation,' declared Arthur Wooster. 'No wonder Michael Wilson asked as soon as he arrived, "How is the crew's morale?"'

ANATOMY OF AN EXPLOSION

The special effects department is central to this kind of filming. Four truckloads of gear, from welding apparatus to water pumps, from engineering machinery to generators, were brought in – all the equipment necessary to undertake any job on the production. Chris Courbould, in charge of special effects in Mexicali, could be seen organizing several things at once – arranging for a towbar to be fixed to a truck to turn it into a tracking vehicle, sending people off to fill up sandbags for an explosion, chasing around for empty containers to fill up with petrol, undertaking small engineering jobs for the tankers or the plane, and generally working on three different sequences at once. In addition to his four English colleagues, Chris had a

Top: *One of the several explosions that indicate the demise of one of Sanchez' trucks.*
Above: *'The transfer' is how the crew refer to the stunt in which Bond drops from the crop-duster on to the top of a fast-moving tanker.*
Right: *A production still showing how one of the sequences of Bond running along the top of the tanker was shot.*

team of nine from Mexico City who had all worked together on several international films, under Laurencio 'Choby' Cardeco, a talkative Mexican who has been in the business for some 39 years.

Special effects tackle every mechanical difficulty on the unit as well as being responsible for all the effects that are seen in front of camera. Fire, smoke, explosions and dust clouds are all the province of this department. A typical problem they faced was how to create fire without smoke. They had to experiment with five different kinds of fuel before they came up with the right answer.

The most spectacular area of their work is creating explosions of the kind that happen when the tankers blow up. John Richardson who, according to Chris, is 'the best big bangs man in the business' planned it but Chris and his team executed it. It can take six or seven hours to prepare one of these explosions. Around 500 gallons of petrol and 50 sticks of dynamite are often used for one large bang. The effect is carefully choreographed using a cocktail of different explosives: gunpowder, dynamite, cortex, petrol and napthalene. Different bombs are prepared – some directional, some that spread out in all directions and oth-

ers which add little bits of finesse. These are then placed in various areas of the tanker and timed to go off within milliseconds of one another. The whole explosion may only take a quarter of a second and the eye may not be able to distinguish the different parts but the overall effect is breathtaking.

When one explosion was filmed, using two remote cameras stationed near to the scene and the main camera a safe distance from it, clouds of black smoke and flames poured from the tanker, setting half the cliff on fire, both above and below it. The heat of the explosion could be felt over 185m (200 yds) away.

Above: *This drawing shows how the explosion of one of the tankers was prepared. Different concoctions of explosive are placed at various sites and then timed to go off within milliseconds of each other. It is a highly complex procedure and each explosion in the film has to be as carefully planned.*

ANATOMY OF AN EXPLOSION

450 Gallons of Petrol   36×802 sticks of dynamite

1 Instantaneous
2 50 Milliseconds Delay
3 100 Milliseconds Delay
4 150 Milliseconds Delay
5 200 Milliseconds Delay
6 2 Second Delay

THE TANKERS

The Kenworth Truck Company of Seattle, Washington, are one of the largest trucking manufacturers in the USA with between 10 and 15 per cent of the market. Their trucks are customised, specially built by their engineers to provide the customers with exactly what they require. They cost from US$65,000 for a basic model to US$120,000 for a deluxe one with a large engine, chrome fittings, portable TV and stereo sound system. Kenworth's association with James Bond began early on in the development of *Licence to Kill* when publicity director Saul Cooper approached the company. Kenworth were interested because of the Bond image. They consider their

Above: *One of the Kenworth trucks had to be especially adapted to perform this stunt – the famous 'side wheelie' from the tanker chase.*

Right: *During one shot, a tanker accidentally crashed into the rocky surround of the road. The effect was so good that they decided to keep it in the film.*

Below: *A camera's eye view of the chase. Rigging the camera in this way provides shots as they might be seen from somebody hanging on to the side of the truck. In other words, it gives Bond's view of the action when he is balancing precariously trying to get into the driver's cabin.*

products the Rolls-Royce of trucks and thought an involvement would complement their image.

However, Kenworth receive many approaches from film companies and are careful about the impression they give on the screen, not wishing to be associated with anything that shows trucks or trucking in a bad light.

They were concerned primarily with the very important issues of safety. When the production team assured them that it was mindful of these concerns, Kenworth agreed to join forces with Bond.

Rémy Julienne, the stunt driver co-ordinator, went to their plant and met a team of engineers to discuss the modifications needed for the trucks to be able to perform the kinds of tricks expected of a Bond chase. He showed them video footage of similar stunts that he had performed in Paris and then the engineers set to work.

Kenworth provided three new trucks specially designed for the film. One was capable of being driven by remote control, with a second steering apparatus hidden in the sleeping compartment. The second was modified so that it could drive on its rear wheels only and the third could perform a similar trick on its side wheels. In each case, working closely with Rémy Julienne, the Kenworth engineers had to modify the suspension, the brakes, the shock absorbers and the steering mechanisms of the trucks.

Kenworth are excited about their involvement in the film – it is one of the biggest public relations exercises that they have ever undertaken. They plan to use a documentary video about the modifications and the stunts for their own promotional purposes.

In addition to the three trucks specially built by Kenworth, the art department found five old Kenworth trucks which they bought and refurbished in Mexico, changing the lights, painting them and adding the chrome to make them interchangeable with the US ones. Twelve tankers, five of them made from wood for the explosions, also had to be assembled. It was a mammoth task for the art department but the sight of the gleaming finished trucks was well worth the effort.

Left: *Dominique Julienne, Rémy's son, has a strange fascination for the more exotic wildlife of the area.*

Right: *Another tanker bites the dust.*

PROFILE

Name: Rémy Julienne

Bond history: *For Your Eyes Only* (vehicle stunt co-ordinator), *Octopussy* (vehicle stunt co-ordinator), *A View to a Kill* (vehicle stunt co-ordinator), *The Living Daylights* (vehicle stunt co-ordinator), *Licence to Kill* (vehicle stunt co-ordinator).

Rémy Julienne began his association with the Bonds in 1980 with the Citroen car chase and the motor-bike fight in the snow in *For Your Eyes Only*. He has since become an integral part of the Bond team. He advises on how best to achieve a given effect in the script, adds suggestions of his own to improve the action and supplies the mechanical and driving expertise to carry it all out. Driving a car down steps to the banks of the Seine (in *A View to a Kill*), or jumping a burning truck over a burning road (in *Licence to Kill*), is in his domain.

He was always present in Mexicali, limping around the set (he had pulled a ligament), speaking halting English (except when talking about car parts) and videoing everything in sight (he uses what he has shot to review the stunts with stop frame to assess the action of his vehicles and his drivers).

Rémy, who was the French Motorcross champion in 1958, has been a stuntman himself since 1964 when he worked on *Fantomas*. He earned an international reputation organizing the driving sequences in *The Italian Job* (1969) and *French Connection II* (1975). At first he worked on his own, then he began to build a team of mechanics and drivers (including his two sons, Dominique and Michel). He has workshops and a testing ground outside Paris where he can experiment with engineering, stunts and techniques.

Nowadays he works around the world, organizing and co-ordinating driving for everything from Japanese TV commercials to a James Bond film. 'The Bond films,' Remy explained, 'are exceptional. They know that we are able to do many things but they also know that we have a limit. They are very easy to work with. John Glen is a great director. I know his ways, his talent – he can do anything.'

Rémy is extremely proud of his work with Bond and wants to do a side-wheelie down the Champs Elysees as part of the promotion for *Licence to Kill*.

The tankers, carrying a mixture of cocaine and gasoline, drive away from the OMI.

THE PLANE

The crop-duster which Bond and Pam fly is a Piper PA-18 Super Cub. It is a utility plane used for border patrols, crop-dusters (as in the film), fish-spotting and recreational purposes. It has short take-off and landing requirements making it convenient for this rocky terrain. But above the 1846m (6000 ft) of the Rumorosa, the air is three times as hot as normal and the plane had a tendency to be sluggish. Breezes, thermals and a fierce wind which whips around the peaks created problems for the plane and its pilots.

One of the most spectacular stunts, known by the crew as 'the transfer', occurs when Bond jumps from the plane on to one of the tankers. To get the timing right took a lot of practice. It needed very still air for the action to happen and the truck had to remain straight when being driven fast. The first time it was tried with 007 in action, he landed spot on and immediately stood up. Everyone was worried that it did not look sufficiently difficult.

The Mexico/US border is a notorious area for drug trafficking and the Mexican authorities were particularly worried when the film unit cleared an area of land for use as an airstrip. Part of the agreement was that when the film left town, they would return the strip to its original condition, complete with fences, to prevent other aircraft from using it. Nevertheless, one day when Corkey Fornof, the pilot, landed there, he found himself surrounded by armed police demanding to search the plane. It was a case of real life imitating the Bond script.

Left: *Four of the tankers wind their way up the spectacular Rumorosa pass.*

*Three shots from the sequence where Bond drops from the crop duster on to the moving truck. Pam flies the lightweight plane (**top**) over a tanker; Bond manoeuvres himself into the right position (**middle**); and finally he waits for the right moment to transfer to the tanker (**bottom**). It is one of the most exciting stunts in the film. The helicopter is the camera platform.*

SPECIAL EFFECTS

Special effects is a bit of a misnomer. It is easy to imagine that this department deals with little else except explosions, fires and smoke. In fact, it is central to all aspects of the filming, concerned with everything that is not actually shot for real. Wind, rain and dust are all created by special effects; they design and create rigs for stunt work; models, miniatures and dummies all fall within their remit.

'We are given a basic script with a lot of the effects in,' explained John Richardson, the head of the department, 'but one of the nice things about the way the Bond family works is that we all have the opportunity to put in ideas.' In *The Living Daylights*, for instance, it was John's sugestion to use miniatures for the parachutes coming out of the back of the Hercules plane when there were problems making the original idea work.

Using the script as a basis, they try to create interesting effects which are Bondish and which work in the right context. From gadgets to bits of trickery that are needed in the sets, this involves working closely with the art department, creating things that fulfil both their requirements. For instance, the Polaroid camera in *Licence to Kill* has to fire a laser. Special effects worked something out which projected a light. John Glen might have said that he wanted a brighter flash or a shorter one and so the concept evolved into something that everybody thought looked best. Then special effects draw it up and the boys in the workshop built it.

Left: *Special effects supervisor John Richardson operates one of his department's guns on board the Wavekrest.*

Below: *The special effects store at Churubusco Studios had enough equipment to start a small factory. They have to be fully geared up to tackle not only all the planned special effects but also numerous unforeseen problems that arise while shooting.*

The special effects department, one of the largest on the film, had 10 people brought specially from England, 15 Mexicans, three Californians and three people from Miami. Most of them are general effects specialists – as John called them 'jacks of all trades, masters of none'. They are all used to working on the floor, all have a good knowledge of pyrotechnics, all are fair welders. In addition there is a good electronics guy, a modelmaker, a radio control man and an engineer who runs the workshop. 'When they heard there was a lot of underwater stuff in this picture, most of the boys went off and took courses. I've been diving myself for over 20 years' John commented.

The equipment is equally impressive – engineering machinery, welders, lathes, milling machines, but, John continued, 'A lot of what we do is fine bench work involving skilled crafts and using hand tools.' Most of the electronic equipment had to be sent from London because it was impossible to get in Mexico. Similarly a lot of the materials were imported, partially because things are much more expensive in Mexico and partially because it could often take days to find exactly what they needed.

The most difficult sequence in *Licence to Kill* for special effects is, of course, the one in Mexicali because it involves so many different stunts, rigs and effects. 'They are not that complex to design but the volume of work involved is enormous,' John commented. He had between 30 and 40 people working in Mexico City, welding, cutting, changing and adapting the tankers and the prime movers that pull them in order to prepare for the shoot.

Above: *Chris Corbould, in charge of special effects in Mexicali, orchestrates his department. While setting up one shot, they would be continually in contact with the main crew, shooting elsewhere, as well as laying plans for the shot after next.*

Left: *Bond runs away from an enormous tanker explosion, carefully engineered by the special effects team.*

Below: *Anthony Zerbe with two latex mock ups of his head which are used in the decompression chamber sequence aboard the* Wavekrest.

The script calls for several of the tankers to be blown up. According to the script, one is hit by a missile, one blows when its fuel is ignited and two go up when they collide. This caused problems for special effects because obviously they did not want to do it the same way several times as this would have been repetitive. They needed to design a number of different spectacular but safe explosions. John Richardson's job was to come up with the ideas of ways to do this and then put it all into practice. For one explosion, for instance, they considered using radio controls, but in the end a stunt driver drove the vehicle while the special effects people hid in the back of the cab and detonated the explosion while the tanker was on the move.

One of special effects' responsibilities is safety. There are no written rules but, as John said, 'Experience determines safety. If I build a rig it is my responsibility to see that it is safe. Also if I have designed a particular rig, I know what the danger points are and the things that could potentially go wrong.'

A new departure for *Licence to Kill*, but not for John, is the scene where Krest explodes in the decompression chamber. John has been involved with make-up and animatronic effects 'ever since I first came into the industry'. First they took a face mould of the actor and created a master mould from which they produced a thin latex skin of the actor's face which fitted over a fibreglass mask. They added fibreglass eyes and teeth and then made it up. Finally, they put various air-pipes and trickery inside the fibreglass. At the given moment the audience can see it start to blow up and the effect is very believable.

On the set, John was everywhere at once, planning, overseeing and actually getting involved in the heavy work that accompanied all the rigs and effects. Sometimes he was even working on two units at once. But, 'I only do 24 hours a day when absolutely necessary,' was his final comment.

PROFILE

Name: John Richardson

Bond History: *Moonraker* (special effects team), *Octopussy* (special effects supervisor), *A View to a Kill* (special effects supervisor), *The Living Daylights* (special effects supervisor), *Licence to Kill* (special effects supervisor).

On being asked how he got into the industry, John Richardson, the special effects supervisor, disarmingly – and honestly – replied, 'Nepotism!' His father, Cliff Richardson, started in the film business in 1921 when they did not have clearly defined special effects departments. He worked in props in the days when they did make-up, lighting and virtually everything. From there he began making gadgets and gimmicks and models before finally pioneering a fully-fledged special effects unit. He invented and developed a lot of the things that are taken for granted today like fog machines and black bursters (a pyrotechnic fire-ball effect). And clearly John is very proud of his father's achievements.

In the late 1950s, when his father was working on *Exodus* (1960), John was 13 or 14 and went on location for three months during the school holidays. 'I got my first job in special effects, got a bit part in the film and ended up in accounts for a time.' He left school in 1962 and immediately went to work for his father on films like *The Victors* (1963). 'I trained in the field,' said John. 'Luckily I had an aptitutde for mechanics.' Through the 1960s he worked on *Help* (1965), *Casino Royale* (1967), and many other films. After *The Dirty Dozen* (1967), father and son were offered two films at once. 'My first film as supervisor was *Duffy*' (1968). They continued to work together on large films like *The Battle of Britain* (1969), and *Young Winston* (1972). 'He would do one unit, I would do the other.'

But at the same time, John was earning his own reputation on films like *Straw Dogs* (1971) and *The Omen* (1976) which was 'the most successful effects pictures I'd done at the time.' *A Bridge Too Far* (1977) was one of his most complex achievements because of its scale and scope – 1.5 tons of high explosive, 20 tons low-explosive, 20,000 motor car tyres for burning, 15,000 gallons of fuel, 100 tons of cement, umpteen miles of twinflex. John also has *Superman* (1978) and five Bonds to his credit. He won an Oscar for *Aliens* (1986) for which he built the power loader that Sigourney Weaver uses to attack the monster mother. It was quite a challenge as it was difficult to build and had to appear to operate. He also had a limited time and a demanding director who worried about the shape of every nut and bolt to cope with.

Cliff, who had worked on several of 'Cubby' Broccoli's early films, and John were going to do a Bond many years ago but something happened. After *Raise the Titanic!* (1980), John was offered *Octopussy*. 'They called and asked if I were free. I was and only too happy to get on to a Bond and I've been part of the family ever since.'

The biggest kick that John Richardson has got out of a Bond film was the opening sequence to *Octopussy* where the tiny AcroStar jet flies into a hangar and blows everything up in its wake. 'I liked it because the whole sequence worked so well with a lot of effects. We were involved in the models, all the other effects, rigs, explosions, building the horse-box, building the aircraft that goes into the horse-box, the hangar blowing up and the missile coming into the hangar. That was the best.

'There were a couple of shots where the jet is chased by a missile. We had a radio-controlled model of the jet which took off with the missile on top, piggy-back style. The missile was attached to a spool of wire inside the model of the aircraft. When the model rolled, the missile rolled off and the wire splayed out from the spool, towing the missile behind the model. So wherever the model flew, the missile followed. It was a difficult but simple idea.'

WHEN THE SHOOTING STOPS

Editor John Grover is working at his Pic-sync in his cutting-room at Pinewood Studios.

All films are made in the cutting-room, they say, for once the shooting has stopped, it is up to the editor to create the film from the footage at his disposal. 'People outside the industry,' explained John Grover, the editor of this and three previous Bonds, 'think that editing is splicing the film together as it actually happens. They have no idea that it is made up, in the case of a Bond film, of thousands of short cuts. We worked out at one time that the average length of a cut was about two seconds.'

The Bond films are particularly fast-moving. American audiences, they argue, are easily bored and so the pace has to be relentless. Nothing – no shot, no stunt and no joke – is ever shown or heard twice. 'The Bond films bash your eyeballs,' is John Grover's description of the style.

'The idea is to entertain,' he continued. 'These are movies for youthfully orientated people.' And everything is done to speed up the action, pausing occasionally for a slower romantic interlude. After director John Glen has taken a master shot of a scene, he proceeds to take the same scene from a number of different angles, providing a lot of cover for the editor to choose from. This allows fast, pacy cutting back and forth between different takes, removing all the breaths, hesitations and pauses.

'People can't actually talk that fast,' John commented. Where sequences, like the underwater scenes, are inherently slow, John frame cuts it to speed it up. In the end, the film moves so fast that 'you have to see it twice to catch all the action.'

John, and his assistant Matthew Glen, started work during the shoot-

PROFILE

Name: John Grover

Bond History: *The Spy Who Loved Me* (assistant editor); *Moonraker* (assembly editor); *For Your Eyes Only* (editor); *Octopussy* (editor); *The Living Daylights* (editor); *Licence to Kill* (editor).

After doing his national service in a tank regiment when he left school at 18, John Grover meant to go to university with the aim of finding a career in insurance. But he joined a film unit in the army as a stills photographer and became interested in the film industry. An uncle who was a film editor told him, 'It's the most marvellous industry to be in but if you want security, forget it. It's very stimulating, you never do the same thing twice and it's a very young industry.' It sounded more interesting than insurance and when John received a phone call offering him a job, he did not hesitate. I never really knew what an editor was, I just knew it was a stimulating industry.'

He moved from Norwich to London in 1959, to earn 6 a week as a trainee. John carries a file around with him, on the back of which his film credits over the years are listed so it was easy to discover that his first job as an assistant, proper, was on *The Secret Partner* starring Stewart Granger. 'I worked on some tremendous movies as an assistant,' John reminisced, 'working with master directors who had previously been editors, like David Lean on *Doctor Zhivago* (1965) or Robert Wise on *The Haunting* (1963).

When John Glen took over the direction of the Bond films on *For Your Eyes Only*, John Grover was offered the chance to edit and, apart from *A View to a Kill* where he could not get out of a previous engagement, he has stayed with the series ever since. 'I do the Bonds for "Cubby", because he gave me the breaks,' he said.

ing. In Mexico and Key West they assemble the film as it comes in, showing rushes, picking out the best takes and assembling some of the sequences. Organisation plays a large part in the editing room at this stage. On a Bond film, an enormous amount of film is shot and it all has to be numbered and coded so that even the smallest offcut of film can be identified.

Dialogue scenes, John estimated are shot at a ratio of 10 or 15:1, while action sequences, where sometimes as many as four cameras are poised to catch the action, is more like 100:1. An estimated 475,000 ft of film was shot between the various units on *Licence to Kill*, a lot of celluloid to sort through.

'The hardest part,' John said, 'is putting it together initially, creating the first assembly, going through all the material, trying to sort out what I consider to be the best parts.' He then shows his assembly to the director who in his turn makes changes to reach what is known as the director's cut.

John Glen was an editor before he went into directing and obviously still enjoys being in the cutting-room and handling the film, though he can be impatient at times. He often asks, 'What else have you got?' His editing experience is invaluable in the detailed pre-planning of the film, particularly the action sequences. In rushes, he is very conscientious, watching everything and giving each unit a detailed report.

The action sequences are so closely storyboarded that the shot order rarely changes in the cutting-room. It is only altered if a sequence does not work. Then, it is either reshot or thrown away. On a Bond, there is no thought of rescuing the film in the cutting-room as many lower-budget movies are forced to do. In *The Living Daylights*, for instance, a scene where Bond escapes from the casbah on a flying carpet was elbowed because it was too slow and did not fit in with the Bond pace.

After rushes comes the first cut which is put together as it is being filmed. At this stage, *Licence to Kill* returned to Pinewood Studios in England. Cyril Howard, the Studio

From each Bond film, an out-take movie is compiled of all the daft and amusing moments on the set when people forget their lines, fool around or get the action wrong. The film, which the whole crew collude in putting together, is a traditional highspot at the end of picture party.

Head from Pinewood welcomed the film back.

'It was a great sadness when Bond took off for Mexico,' he commented. 'For us, they are like an institution, a hardy perennial. It's not the same without a Bond in the calendar. I'm happy they are back.'

By Christmas 1988, four weeks after the end of the shoot, some sequences had already been set. The sequences are rough-dubbed with all the effects in place and set to music as the editors go along giving them a clear idea of how it might work in the end. 'This is good for the picture,' John explained, 'because you know the sequence isn't going to fall flat when its finished.'

John, who had at this stage seen more of the film than anybody, added a comment about the Mexican location. 'It will be very interesting to see if this Bond will be like the previous ones or whether it will lose its English flavour'.

In *Octopussy*, there was one stunt that all of the cameras missed. A Beechcraft plane going over a cliff did not explode where it was intended to but crashed behind a hill. All the cameras recorded was a whiff of smoke.

Left: *Keith Hamshere, one of the unit stills photographers, in action during the filming of the wedding sequence. At one point it looked as if Keith would have to feature in the film as wedding photographer.*

Below right: *'Jerry' Juroe (seated) and Saul Cooper on location.*

MUSIC

Michael Kamen, the composer of the music for *Licence to Kill*, is one of the newest members of the Bond team. He takes over from John Barry who has worked on 11 previous Bonds. 'Cubby' Broccoli and Michael Wilson said, 'we are pleased to welcome Michael Kamen to our team.'

Michael Kamen may be new to Bond but he is no stranger to film music. His credits include *Die Hard* (1988), *Lethal Weapon* (1987), *Brazil* (1985) and the British television thriller, 'The Edge of Darkness'. New York-born Michael studied oboe at the world famous Julliard School of Music before forming the New York Rock Ensemble which gained fame in the mid-Sixties at campuses and concert halls across America. He has worked with a diverse range of bands including Pink Floyd, the Eurythmics and Queen, as well as composing a full-length ballet score – Rodin Mis En Vie –for the Harkness Ballet.

For Michael 1989 is a bumper year. Apart from *Licence to Kill*, he has written the scores for *Adventures of Baron Munchausen, Raggedy Rawney* starring Bob Hoskins and Joel Silver's *Roadhouse* starring Patrick Swayze.

PROFILE

Name: Maurice Binder

Bond history: *Dr No, Thunderball, You Only Live Twice, On Her Majesty's Secret Service, Diamonds Are Forever, Live and Let Die, The Man With the Golden Gun, The Spy Who Loved Me, Moonraker, For Your Eyes Only, Octopussy, A View to a Kill, The Living Daylights, Licence to Kill* (all as main title designer).

Maurice Binder has designed most of the main titles of the Bond movies, including the famous Bond gunbarrel logo used to introduce every film. He was offered the job on *Dr No* after his titles for Stanley Donen's *The Grass is Greener* which featured several cuddly babies on a lawn representing the actors and technicians of the credits. Binder's hallmarks – beautiful girls and a touch of eroticism – have adorned the titles of nearly all the subsequent Bond films. He once again brings his unique talents to the main title of *Licence to Kill*.

MARKETING

Marketing (the publicising, advertising and promotion of a product or company) has always been one of the most important aspects of the Bond films over the years. It is considered to be a key element in the continuing success of the series.

Charles 'Jerry' Juroe is the worldwide head of marketing for the Bond films. In practice, this means that he and/or his associates, Saul Cooper and Derek Coyte, are responsible for co-ordinating all aspects of 'selling' *Licence to Kill* during both its production and distribution phases. Working in close conjunction with the marketing departments at MGM/UA in California and United International Pictures in London, these members of the Bond team are party to the decisions that concern making the public aware that a new 007 film is on the drawing board, in the pipeline and, finally, ready to hit the silver screen.

Jerry is among the handful of people still involved with the series who were associated with Bond since the beginning. When *Dr. No* went into production, he was the head of European publicity at United Artists, for whom the film was made. He still remembers his first Bond publicity stunt when he took Sean Connery on a promotional tour of Italy. While there they went to a casino near Turin and he arranged with the management for the new 007 to 'break the bank'. 'Happily, the story broke big all over the world,' he says.

The second key member of the promotion team is Saul Cooper, another Bond veteran who handled the publicity on *The Spy Who Loved Me* and who was associated with several of the Bond films when he was an executive at United Artists in New York and Paris.

While Jerry is based in London during the post-production and pre-release time frames, Saul handles matters from his Los Angeles base. Obviously, they are in constant communication and both have said they would like to meet the inventor of the fax machine to thank him for making life so much easier.

From pre-production through to final release in every major country, the marketing plans are formulated between the Bond team and the two distribution companies. Two or three typical examples are: which journalists visit the set; which photographs are good enough for circulation; the creative development of trailers and posters that first introduce the film.

An important part of the publicity activity during the shoot is the photographic coverage of the film. This provides stills that tell the story of the film or show the behind-the-scenes activity. Two photographers worked on the two units, making this photographic record. Both Keith Hamshere and George Whitear have been with the Bonds for many years and their photographs provide the basis for all the reportage which appear in newspapers and magazines. Also, many of the posters and even books (like this one) about the film, feature their work. At Churubusco, Keith set up his own photographic studio in the corner of one of the stages, in order to take many of the more posed, glamour shots for which the Bond publicity is justly famous.

During the filming, a special video crew was brought in to make a behind-the-scenes publicity documentary, shooting the unit while they were shooting the film. Costing well over $100,000 to film and edit, the video will be used in all kinds of ways from excerpts on television programmes to a promotional film for Kenworth Trucks.

The press themselves, while extremely necessary to Bond publicity, provide some of the biggest headaches for the department during shooting. A Bond film is always international news and 'journalists' eager to get the latest bit of gossip into the tabloids are often found around the unit. Unfounded rumours swing from luxury villas to terrorist threats and this appears in the press as the gospel truth! Other, more reputable media people needed information too and the stars of the film were constantly requested to do yet another interview or photo session.

Another aspect of the department is merchandising: the promotion and licensing of official Bond products. This is done in conjunction with Glidrose Publications, who own the Bond publishing rights and half the merchandising rights. That falls under the remit of Derek Coyte, a former head of publicity at Pinewood Studios, who has long been associated with the series. Around the world, everything from jogging suits to board games has been manufactured under licence at one time or another. One of the most bizarre products ever was a special edition Citroen 2CV with the 007 gun logo on the side, complete with bullet holes, which went on sale to mark the release of *For Your Eyes Only*. For *Licence to Kill* activity is more traditional; a novelisation of the film, written by John Gardner who already has seven James Bond novels to his credit, major commitments with such diverse companies as Sterling Motorcars, Martini and three books with Hamlyn, including this one.

Two of the glamour shots that are traditionally a hallmark of the Bond publicity. **Above:** *Benicio del Toro who plays Dario.* **Right:** *Robert Davi and Talisa Soto in the sort of shot that will be used in colour magazines around the world to promote the film.* **Opposite:** *Aerospatiele provided helicopters for use on* Licence to Kill *and have had a long association with the Bond films.*

PROFILE

Name: 'Jerry' Juroe

Bond history: *Moonraker, For Your Eyes Only, Octopussy, A View to a Kill, The Living Daylights,* and *Licence to Kill* (as head of publicity).

Charles 'Jerry' Juroe is among the handful of people that have been associated with the Bond films since the beginning. When *Dr No* went into production, he was the head of European publicity at United Artists, for whom the film was made. He still remembers when just before the release of *Dr No* he took Sean Connery to a casino in Northern Italy and arranged with the management for the new 007 to 'break the bank'. The stunt resulted in worldwide media coverage.

'Jerry' had his first brush with show-business during the war when he was in the special services after VE day where he found himself handling shows headlining entertainers like Bob Hope, Jack Benny and Ingrid Bergman. Later on he worked in the publicity department of Paramount Studios, during the Golden Age of the early Fifties. He left Hollywood to go to Europe in 1956 with Marilyn Monroe, where she made *The Prince and the Showgirl* with Sir Laurence Olivier. He found he rather liked England and has been largely based in Europe ever since.

He has had various high-level publicity and advertising jobs in the industry, including handling the foreign release of Cecil B DeMille's *The Ten Commandments* and reckons he was 'in the right place at the right time' when the Bond series started. He stayed with United Artists for the first five 007 films and then left to go into production. He returned to the fold with *The Man With the Golden Gun* and has worked full-time for 'Cubby' Broccoli since *Moonraker*. Jerry is now Senior Vice-President of his U.S. company, Warfield Productions.

Licence to Kill will be his last Bond film full-time. However, he has agreed to remain as a part-time consultant on the next movie.

CAST LIST

LICENCE TO KILL

CREDITS

Albert R. Broccoli presents

James Bond	Timothy Dalton
Pam Bouvier	Carey Lowell
Franz Sanchez	Robert Davi
Lupe Lamore	Talisa Soto
Milton Krest	Anthony Zerbe
Sharkey	Frank McRae
Killifer	Everett McGill
Joe Butcher	Wayne Newton
Darlo	Benicio del Toro
Truman-Lodge	Anthony Starke
President Hector Lopez	Pedro Armendariz
Q	Desmond Llewelyn
Felix Leiter	David Hedison
Della Churchill	Priscilla Barnes
M	Robert Brown
Miss Moneypenny	Caroline Bliss
Heller	Don Stroud
Hawkins	Grand L. Bush
Kwang	Cary-Hiroyuki Tagawa
Perez	Alejandro Bracho
Braun	Guy de Saint Cyr
Mullens	Rafer Johnson
Loti	Diana Lee-Hsu
Fallon	Christopher Neame
Alvarez	Gerardŏ Moreno
Stripper	Jeannine Bisignano
Anna Rack	Marye Morgan
Montelongo	Claudia Brook
Consuela	Cynthia Fallon
Rasmussen	Enrique Novi
Oriental	Osami Kawawo
Chief Chemist	Honorato Magaioni
Wavekrest Captain	Roger Cudney
Sanchez's Chauffeur	Fidel Carriga
Tanker Driver	Jose Abdala
Airport Ticket Agent	Teresa Blake
Casino Manager	Juan Pelaez
Pit Boss	Jorge Russek
Cigarette Boat Owner	Bud Williams
Assistant Hotel Manager	Humberto Elizondo
Producers	Albert R. Broccoli
	Michael G. Wilson
Director	John Glen
Written by	Michael G. Wilson
	Richard Maibaum
Associate Producers	Tom Pevsner
	Barbara Broccoli
Second Unit Director	
and Cameraman	Arthur Wooster
Production Designer	Peter Lamont
Director of Photography	Alec Mills
Composer	Michael Kamen
Special Effects Supervisor	John Richardson
Editor	John Grover
Costume Designer	Jodie Tillen
Casting	Jane Jenkins
	Janet Hirshenson
Production Supervisor	Anthony Waye
Production Accountant	Douglas Noakes
Stunt Supervisor	Paul Weston

Underwater Director	
and Cameraman	Ramon Bravo
Vehicle Stunt Supervisor	Rémy Julienne
Aerial Co-ordinator	'Corkey' Fornof
Parachute Stunt Co-ordinator	B. J. Worth
First Assistant Directors	Miguel Gil
	Miguel Lima
Marketing Director	Charles Juroe
Production Supervisor (Mexico)	Hector Lopez
Production Executive (Key West)	Ned Kopp
Production Manager	Philip Kohler
Production Manager (Mexico)	Efren Flores
Unit Manager	Iris Rose
Aerial Cameraman	Phil Pastuhov
Camera Operator	Michael Frift
Script Supervisor	June Randall
Sound Mixer	Edward Tise
Boom Operator	Martin Trevis
Electrical Supervisor	John Tythe
Supervising Art Director	Michael Lamont
Set Decorator	Michael Ford
Construction Manager	Tony Graysmark
Art Director	Dennis Bosher
Art Director (Key West)	Ken Court
Publicity Director	Saul Cooper
Stills Photographer	Keith Hamshere
Second Assistant Director	Callum McDougall
Camera Focus	Frank Elliott
Camera Grip	Chunky Huse
Make-up Supervisors	George Frost
	Naomi Dunne
Chief Hairdresser	Tricia Cameron
Assembly Editor	Matthew Glen
Sound Editor	Vernon Messenger
Production Co-ordinator	Loolee Deleon
London Contact	Amanda Schofield
Los Angeles Contact	Linda Brown
Costume Supervisors	Barbara Scott
	Hugo Pena
Accountant	Jane Meagher
Production Buyer	Ron Quelch
Property Master	Bert Hearn
Sketch Artist	Roger Deer
Standby Propman	Bernard Hearn
Transport Manager	Arthur Dunne

SECOND UNIT

First Assistant Director	Terry Madden
Camera Operator	Malcolm Macintosh
Continuity	Sue Field
Special Effects Supervisor	Chris Corbould
Stills Photographer	George Whitear
Camera Focus	Michael Evans
Camera Grip	Ken Atherfold
Second Assistant Director	Marcia Gay
Make-up/Hair	Di Holt
Standby Propman	Rodney Pincott
Stunt Arranger	Marc Boyle

INDEX

Figures in italics refer to captions; headings in inverted commas indicate characters in the film.